BREAK
○─○─○─○─○─○THE○─○─○─○─○
CHAINS

WITH CREDIT TIPS AND SECRETS FROM YOUR CREDIT GURU

MALIK DAVIS

For bulk order requests, visit www.MalikDavis.com

For credit restoration or to contact the author visit www.YourCreditGuru.net and www.MalikDavis.com

Publishing Coordination by Brown & Duncan Brand, LLC. BandDBrand.com

Printed in the United States of America

ISBN: 978-1-7324971-0-8

Disclaimer: The information in this book has been compiled based on public information and author experience, which has not been subject to an audit or review engagement. Accordingly, the author nor publishers accept any responsibility for the reliability, accuracy or completeness of the compiled financial information nor do we accept liability of any kind whatsoever, including liability by reason of negligence, to any person for losses incurred as a result of placing reliance on the compiled financial information. The information provided in this book, including but not limited to its opinion and analyses, is based on financial data believed to be reliable but is not guaranteed, represented or warranted to be complete. The charts depict the results of our research and are not influenced by any other factors except the information available at the time of printing. Your use of any information from this book is at your own risk and without recourse against the author, publisher, or their employees and content providers. A complete list of sources from this book is located at the end.

DEDICATION

For my heavenly grandmother, Mrs. Annie Cowan Collins Tisdale,
who raised me as one of her own, I know that you are proud and smiling
down on me right now.

To my wife Tiffaney,
You manage to be supportive through all of my trials and tribulations.
You have been an inspiration in my life.
If it were not for you and your patience, I would not be where I am today.
I owe a lot of my success to you.

"Beside every great man stands his woman.
There is no greater man than the man that can acknowledge the woman
standing right next to him."- **Author Rachel Wolchin**

TESTIMONIALS

"One of the reasons why my credit is incredible is because of Malik Davis, the credit guru. It's real, it's no joke. Your credit is your bank."
Toni Braxton

"I'm in a place in my life where I want people to be better; physically, financially, emotionally and spiritually. If you are really sick and tired of high interest rates and trying to establish credit and get your credit where it needs to be, you need to call the brother Malik Davis the credit guru. He's amazing!"
Isaac Carree, Gospel Artist

"... Malik has access to all three credit bureaus. He goes in there, and if you [have] evictions, if you have all kinds of random things from ten to fifteen years of college loans lingering on your credit, keeping your credit score down, he goes in and cleans up everything. He did it for me."
Tyrese Gibson, R&B Artist and Entertainer

"My credit had gotten so bad that I got turned down for a magazine subscription. I called my guy Malik Davis, and he is the top credit guru. He got me straight; my credit is way up. I feel extremely blessed and excited about my future. I vouch for him. Not only did he get me straight, but he got some of my family members straight."
James Fortune, Gospel Artist

"My credit was not always perfect. The only reason I could buy bars was not because I'm rich, but because my man the Credit Guru Malik Davis fixed my score. He took me out of the toilet; I was below 500 and he put me over 800."
OG Peter Thomas, Entrepreneur and Reality Television Star

BREAK THE CHAINS

Don't let poor credit keep you in bondage.

Dear Reader,

Before you start this book, let me keep it real with you for a moment. I get tons of inquiries from people who want me to help them clean up their credit. While, it's my pleasure to help others break the chains of the bad credit blues, let me be honest and say that for most people, a credit repair company should not be necessary. The only time you should use one is if the company is truly able to perform services you can't do, or do not have time to do on your own. Most credit problems can be solved on your own. While disputing errors can be time consuming and responsible credit use isn't instantaneously reflected in your score, the credit-boosting tips and secrets in this book are straight forward.

If you can't find the time or do not want to deal with the credit bureaus, you can pay for professional help. I recommend that you try to fix your credit issues on your own. If you continue to struggle with the credit bureaus and they refuse to remove credit mistakes or you find the job to be too tedious, then you should consider hiring a credit professional, such as myself.

Rebuilding while you repair

It's important to remember that credit repair is usually one step (often the first one) you take when you want to build your way to a better credit score. So, while the repair process may only take **three to six months**, the time it takes to rebuild your credit can take longer.

About the format of this book

After I introduce you to myself and share a little bit of my journey into the world of finances and credit reports, the book gets right down to business. Review the **Credit Vocabulary** at the beginning to make sure you are familiar with the terms that we're going to discuss in this book. Next, work through the book chapter-by-chapter. At the end, you'll find helpful letters that will empower you to begin cleaning up your credit and removing all of the erroneous and inaccurate information from your credit report.

If you follow the tips included within the pages inside, I'm confident that you'll see your credit score begin to increase within a matter of months. Are you ready to break the chains?

Let's go!

-Malik D.

TABLE OF CONTENTS

INTRODUCTION

Have you ever found yourself unable to get financing, rent an apartment, secure a job, or purchase big items such as furniture or appliances because of poor credit? Do you find yourself in a financial hole that you just can't seem to climb out of because of a lack of credit? Do you feel like you are in financial bondage and your hands are chained because your poor credit has been holding you back? Do you need help breaking those chains and overcoming your financial woes, but are clueless about where and how to get started?

What if you had the knowledge and power in the palm of your hands that could help you improve your credit report and scores? What if this knowledge was able to qualify you to purchase your dream home, car, or to achieve some of your other goals? If you haven't been able to get a solid hold on your financial situation and are now looking to break away from the chains that have held you back, then this book is for **YOU!**

Break the Chains includes tips and secrets to help you get back on the road to recovery and regain your financial freedom. I'm excited to help you discover credit repair strategies that the pros use. You will also learn what factors affect your credit score along with short and long-term strategies for fixing your credit. In addition, this book will teach you how to have negative items removed from your credit report and additional resources that can help you in the process. In the back, there's a handy library of letters to help you dispute any items on your credit report.

Breaking the chains requires a lifestyle change. That means becoming a wise money manager, which includes everything from spending, saving, and being smart when it comes to credit utilization. Credit utilization is the amount of credit you have used compare to how much credit you have available (note: this is an important term that I'll mention again). Think of this as the total revolving credit amount you have available by how much you are using. Your credit utilization rate accounts for thirty percent of your overall credit score. Given the significant impact it has on your credit score, you should strive to make your credit utilization rate impressive.

I want you to see that you can start from anywhere and still become successful in your financial life. I did, and you can too. I receive hundreds of messages on a weekly basis from people who are experiencing credit issues, and I needed a way to help everyone, despite not being able to speak one-on-one with everyone who sends me messages. I hope that this book touches everyone who is in bondage to poor credit. **Consider this your credit manual.** It's not a book that you read once and put down. This information is so important that you'll want to revisit certain sections as you face different scenarios in your journey to an excellent credit score (750 or above).

Unfortunately, it is estimated that over eighty million Americans are living with poor credit, and recent studies have shown that up to seventy-nine percent of all credit reports contain errors. That alone is a key reason why I wanted to write this book. Errors and wrongly reported information are costing many of our counterparts valuable points from their credit scores.

Several years ago, certain information on credit scores were kept a secret from consumers. Many people were in the blind about the items on their credit reports until they were denied for a credit card or received an unpleasant letter from a collections agency. The car salesman or finance guy were able to look at your credit report, but you were denied access to your own credit report and the information in it. Some lenders to this day still do not make this available to their customers. Luckily, nowadays there are sites such as Credit Karma, AnnualCreditReport.com, and Credit Sesame that offer free glimpses of updated credit bureau reports. Consumers can also take advantage of a monthly credit monitoring product such as Pro Credit (at www.yourcreditguru.net) to monitor their credit on a monthly or even a daily basis. Technology can help us stay on top of credit issues, which means there are no more excuses. If you aren't happy with your credit score now, decide today that you will make a change. With this book and the resources that you're going to gain, you can become your own credit guru. Negative information on your credit not only affects your purchasing power, but it also has an impact on other key areas of your life, which we will discuss later.

One of the biggest hurdles to financial success is a feeling of being powerless. If you go through the process of reading this book and you still feel that way, then all the advice you read (or hear anywhere else) will seem pretty useless. Instead of inspiring you, it can make you feel like giving up. But don't give up! If you don't take anything else away from this book, I want you to walk away KNOWING that no matter what situation you are in, there is a way to repair your credit and break the chains.

I have good news! With my book, you will be able to take your credit situation into your own hands and begin making small steps towards rebuilding your credit. If it seems a little intimidating or you just don't have the time to go at it alone, consider the option of retaining my professional financial expertise to help you break the chains of financial bondage. Make sure that you're ready for a serious change, because both of our time is valuable, and my services will be an investment for you.

This book is not only going to help you take your credit situation into your own hands and begin making changes, but if you need help, I will take you into my world of credit and you will learn how I can help through your process.

You do not have to continue to be a victim and prisoner of your past credit mistakes. I'll give you the keys to break the shackles and take control of your credit by exercising your legal right to clean up your credit and restore your good name. By using the methods in my book which are modeled after certified credit pros like myself, you can succeed in repairing your own credit. With a high FICO score, you will qualify for the best financing and save thousands of dollars in interest.

Depending on where you are and your credit/financial background, you will be able to determine the best ways to start improving your financial outlook. My simple steps to help improve your credit include:

1) teaching you the key points about the U.S. credit system,

2) obtaining copies of your credit reports and scores, and

3) making sense of the data.

Break the Chains with Credit Tips and Secrets will walk you through this process in a way that is both easy and enlightening. You will learn important inside information that the banks and credit bureaus don't want you to know.

Are you ready to become your own "Credit Guru" and see if you can wear my size eleven shoes? If so, let's get to work.

- **Malik D**.

CREDIT VOCABULARY

Bankruptcy

A proceeding in U.S. Bankruptcy Court that may legally release a person from repaying debts owed. Credit reports normally include bankruptcies for up to ten years.

Charge-off

The balance on a credit obligation that a lender no longer expects to be repaid and writes off as a bad debt.

Collection

Attempted recovery of a past-due credit obligation by a collection department or agency.

Consumer Credit File

A credit bureau record on a given individual. It may include: consumer name, address, Social Security number, credit history, inquiries, collection records, and public records such as bankruptcy filings and tax liens.

Credit Bureau

A credit reporting agency that is a clearinghouse for information on the credit ratings of individuals or firms. Is often called a "credit repository" or a "consumer reporting agency." The three largest credit bureaus in the U.S. are Equifax, Experian, and TransUnion.

CREDIT VOCABULARY

Credit Bureau Risk Score

A type of credit score based solely on data stored at the major credit bureaus. It offers a snapshot of a consumer's credit risk at a particular point in time; it rates the likelihood that the consumer will repay debts as agreed.

Credit History

A record of how a consumer has repaid credit obligations in the past.

Credit Obligation

An agreement by which a person is legally bound to pay back borrowed money or used credit.

Credit Report

Information communicated by a credit reporting agency that bears on a consumer's credit standing. Most credit reports include: consumer name, address, credit history, inquiries, collection records, and any public records such as bankruptcy filings and tax liens.

Credit Risk

The likelihood that an individual will pay his or her credit obligations as agreed. Borrowers who are more likely to pay as agreed pose less risk to creditors and lenders.

Credit Score

This term is often used to refer to credit bureau risk scores. It broadly refers to a number generated by a statistical model which is used to objectively evaluate information that pertains to making a credit decision. Credit scores generally range from 300 to 850.

Default

A failure to make a loan or debt payment when due. Usually an account is considered to be "in default" after being delinquent for several consecutive 30-day billing cycles.

Delinquent

A failure to deliver even the minimum payment on a loan or debt payment on or before the time agreed. Accounts are often referred to as 30, 60, 90 or 120-days delinquent because most lenders have monthly payment cycles.

Equal Credit Opportunity Act (ECOA)

Federal legislation that prohibits discrimination in credit. The ECOA originally was enacted in 1974 as Title VII of the Consumer Credit Protection Act.

Fair Credit Reporting Act (FCRA)

Federal legislation that promotes the accuracy, confidentiality and proper use of information in the files of every "consumer reporting agency." The FCRA was enacted in 1970.

FICO® Scores

Credit bureau risk scores produced from models developed by Fair Isaac Corporation are commonly known as FICO Scores. FICO Scores are used by lenders and others to assess the credit risk of prospective borrowers or existing customers, in order to help make credit and marketing decisions. These scores are derived solely from the information available on credit bureau reports.

Inquiry

An item on a consumer's credit report that shows that someone with a "permissible purpose" (under FCRA rules) has previously requested a copy of the consumer's report. Fair Isaac credit bureau risk scores take into account only inquiries resulting from a consumer's application for credit.

Installment Debt

Debt to be paid at regular times over a specified period. Examples of installment debt include most mortgage and auto loans.

Insurance Bureau Score

An insurance rating based solely on credit bureau data stored at the major credit bureaus. It offers a snapshot of an individual's insurance risk at a particular point in time, and helps insurers evaluate new and renewal auto and homeowner insurance policies.

Late Payment

A delinquent payment; a failure to deliver a loan or debt payment on or before the time agreed.

Revolving Debt

Debt owed on an account that the borrower can repeatedly use and pay back without having to reapply every time credit is used. Credit cards are the most common type of revolving account.

Scoring Model

A statistical formula that is used, usually with the help of computers, to estimate future performance of prospective borrowers and existing customers. A scoring model calculates scores based on data such as information on a consumer's credit report.

These terms will be re-introduced throughout the book to empower you with the language that you need to *Break the Chains.*

MALIK DAVIS

CHAPTER 1

How I Became the Credit Guru

Before I got involved in the credit business, I was deeply embedded into a dangerous lifestyle on the streets of Chicago. I grew up where news of homicide, interacting with junkies, and witnessing drug deals were not uncommon. For most people around me, we had one of two choices: live or die. To live often meant we had to risk our lives or figure out a clever way to survive. It was indeed "survival of the fittest." My early childhood paved the way to a life that was dangerous because it demanded me to survive, and in order to do so, I had to learn the necessary survival skills. Sadly, this is far too common for many black youth, especially those who live (or grew up) in this nation's inner city neighborhoods.

I lived in North Chicago with four siblings and a hard-working mother, who worked for the government to make ends meet for us. I know she loved us and did the best she could to raise us as a single parent, however, the environment sucked us in. Although she hated it, she had no control over the affect the inner-city life had on us. You see, the streets were quite welcoming to youth like me, and it often felt like we had no choice but to look for a better life through a street system set up by design. This system trained us to seek fast money.

As you can imagine, the story went as follows: my mother's "good government job" couldn't quite meet our family's needs. Eventually, I felt I had no choice but to accept the enticing "job offer" the streets had on the table. I found myself and family hungry and destitute after our mom could not carry the heavy load and pay all the bills alone. I was the oldest, the man of the house, and I felt I had to find ways to help. We needed money fast, and as a man, I was going to figure out a way to make sure my family ate. You see, pain and suffering through the eyes of children causes them to take the responsibilities of adults. While I'm sure my mom did not want me to do so, our life at home drove me to look for a remedy quick. If you've never been in these shoes before, then count yourself seriously blessed. As I said, the streets were made readily available by design to offer black kids jobs. It gave us positions as distributors of manufactured goods. Mostly blacks, some whites, and other races, were sucked into this trap. With little experience and no references, we just needed to fit the job description. As I look back in hindsight, the only qualifications that we had to meet were that of destitute children who were hungry for money and willing to hustle hard at this entry-level opportunity. I said, "yes" to the job offered to me, and I was hired on the spot. I was a natural born hustler, and the money came to me quickly.

22

HOW I BECAME THE CREDIT GURU

Back at home, my mom was a holy woman of God who would not have approved of what I *had* to do. She took us along with her to church each weekend, and I was inspired on Sundays and sometimes even on Wednesday nights during bible study too. However, no amount of "inspiration" in church changed our financial situation or rescued me from my new employer. In my eyes, the religious buildings (on practically every corner) could not pay bills. Besides, I was now a young Boss. I wasn't about to wait for a special day to come to receive a handout from the church. I wasn't looking for handouts. Chicago taught me to get it on my own, and do what I had to do to take care of home. My family needed to eat NOW. Bills were piling up; we were hungry, and I couldn't find a pastor volunteering to step in and be a partner to my mom in providing for our family. I did what I had to do for us. Prayers just didn't seem to be answered quick enough, so the church couldn't save me from this street life. I was inside a world with savages, and it was up to me not to be eaten alive.

There is an old cliché that says, "When you find out what a person is hungry for, then you feed it to them." Needless to say, the streets did just that. This system's design was to keep the young black male hungry. People also say, "If it ain't broke, don't fix it." Chicago has turned into a war grounds for many 21st century youth today, because to the powers that be, this system is not broken enough to fix. I hate to put such a grim perspective on the city, but there is so much that can be done (in inner cities all over the country), and yet, for some reason, young black lives aren't important enough to fix the system that keeps them down. It still works today for those who designed it. Everybody is getting a piece of the pie—a "justice" system complete with police officers, prosecutors, and judges lock up black men by the busloads; retirement is good for members of this system.

Meanwhile, the younger (and older) generations are falling for the mirage of "street success" every day. This was a problem that we could not see with our desperate hearts, especially as children. I was fed the promise of "success" by entrapment from those at the top. I never saw these people with my natural eyes, but I always knew they existed. Those masterminds were somewhere out there away from reach safely hidden from the common folk. We were never educated about the game of life and death that we faced. They dangled the so-called promise of success in our faces, and my dreams of instant success turned into nightmares of fear and the stench of death all around me. Friends were killed, associates were robbed. Everyone ended up either in jail or dead.

I am here to tell you this story today, so apparently, God loved and wanted me and my siblings alive, despite my blindness. Our prayers were answered, even though His response seemed late to me at the time. They say hindsight is twenty-twenty, and I see now, what I could not see then. This story could go on and on, but I will save it for another book about the story of my life. Long story short, I ended up in prison at an early age.

I didn't know my father, and didn't have a male figure to guide me on how to be a real man. The strong women in the family were our guides and still are. The missing element in many African American families is the father figure. So many boys and young men are deprived of that strong male role model inside of the home, and it has detrimental effects. Many fathers are out living their own lives and forsaking their families, while other men are six feet in the ground or behind bars. Unfortunately, sons are repeating this curse passed down from their fathers. The "get rich quick" idea that society brainwashes us with takes generations after generations down destructive paths. It's time to man up and take responsibility for our lives, in an intelligent way, and stop getting sucked into the traps.

I believe these problems in our country—the breakdown of the family and community structures, are the foundation for our imprisonment. In order to break the chains, we have to mend the family links, fathers must step up, community leaders need to be made accountable, and young people need to be empowered mentally, emotionally, socially, and financially.

I desperately wanted to be the change and switch up the narrative, even at a young age. I may have been in the streets, but I tried my best to be the man that my father wasn't. Before going to jail, I met my wife when I was sixteen-years-old. We married when she was twenty-one and I was twenty-years-old. When we first met, I was living in a group home. I saw her in a downtown mall and we've been making history together ever since.

I didn't tell her where I lived at first, because her parents were very prestigious. Her father held an upper management position at a big energy company and her mother was a minister and well-known gospel radio personality. I learned from other people that her mom was with both local radio and television ministries. I actually used to watch the television ministry her mom was with while I was incarcerated. She was a local counselor for the well-known national 700 Club founded by Evangelist Pat Robinson from Virginia Beach, Virginia. She also served as an ordained minister at a small church. I never wanted her to know my background for fear that she would never accept a street guy like me for her beautiful daughter.

I remember when I first went to visit my wife and my fears became a reality. Her mother, who is now my mother-in-law, was working in her flower garden. When she looked up and saw me with my swag—hat turned backwards—she looked amazed and appalled at the same time. I really did not know how to present myself to a minister, and I felt awkward, afraid, and full of mixed emotions. I wanted to make a good impression, but didn't know how to make that happen. I had hopes of marrying her daughter someday, but she had high hopes for her daughter too. They were higher than mine from the impression I made. She did not accept me and wanted us to break it off, immediately.

From that point on, my girlfriend and I were forced to sneak around. All of our sneaking around eventually caught up to us, because soon, she ended up pregnant. Once I became a permanent fixture in her life, her mom and dad found out that I was in a group home, and this was big trouble for me. They both came over to see me after hearing the news. They were very angry, hurt, and upset. We also had to face the possibility of us having a child while I lived in a group home. It was a difficult decision and her mother didn't believe in abortions, so my wife ended up keeping the baby. With a baby on the way, and despite anyone's opinions, my girl and I were in love. I wanted to be a man, take care of my responsibilities, and marry her. I was excited (and scared) about our new family, but I wanted a family. I wanted to be a father, and I didn't want to leave my child as my dad had done to me. Eventually, they gave in, and my soon-to-be in-laws permitted me to marry their first born daughter.

While I was young, I made big mistakes trying to prove myself with no direction and little experience at being such a young father. We soon had three children to care for, and money was very tight. We had to live with my in-laws. I wanted to be a man and provide for my family, so I turned to what I knew best—the streets. That decision cost me five years, because I violated my probation which landed me in that group home years earlier. I already felt like I had failed my mother when I was a youngin' on the streets of Chicago, and now although at this point, I was in Charlotte, North Carolina, living a new life, I was faced with the familiar feeling of failure all over again. My mother (who I had failed as a teenager) began sacrificing much of her hard-earned money to bail me out of jail. The judge had no leniency for me or my young family, and my worst nightmares came true. I had to spend all five years of the probation violation locked behind bars. I was no longer free to raise my family. This took a huge toll on us all, physically and mentally. My son was not even a year old yet, so the next time I would see him would be during his kindergarten year. I never had a chance to bond with my own son while he was a baby. I had a few years with my daughters, but my son would spend the first few years of his life without a father.

My decision to return to the streets was a bad investment with no return. You see I never got rich in the street game. The people at the top owned the airplanes to transport drugs and plant them in our communities. Hungry, ignorant, drug dealers at the bottom and the blind public who buy and get hooked on drugs fill the graveyards and the prisons. As a man, I wanted to find a way to help my family survive. I did not want them to go through what I did in Chicago. Instead of providing a better way, it seemed I was caught in a cycle of the working poor. My nine-to-five job did not pay enough to get ahead. It was a similar and all too familiar situation. No matter how hard I worked, just like my mom's job, my employment could not provide a decent life for our family. I tried to work and so did my wife. She was also in college while caring for our three children. She never approved of my quick fixes, because she was raised with a mom who was not only a minister, but who also worked in the banking industry. Her stepdad had an auto body shop where I could have worked, but because of my big ego, I chose to return to what I knew—the streets. While I was in jail living through the consequences of my bad decisions, I almost lost my wife. Five years was a long time to ask such a beautiful young woman to wait.

After returning home, I had to win her back. I wanted to change my whole outlook on life so that I would never ever lose her or be away from my family again. I had to have a true plan and a changed mind and heart, or else possibly face death if I returned to the streets again. Worse than death was the broken heart I felt knowing that she could slip away.

Upon arriving home, I received some good news from my wife's grandmother, who was the matriarch of their family. She told me that my mother-in-law had great plans for me, so I'd never have to turn to the streets again to support my family.

The Making of a Credit Guru

When I got out of jail in 1998 (the year my son started kindergarten), I was happy to hear that my mother-in-law, who left the banking industry, was now willing to take a chance on me with her new business. This was a breath of fresh air and the positive news I needed to hear. Her loving heart as a minister began to chisel through my hard heart and big ego, and it won me over. I knew if I failed this time and thought about returning to the streets, I'd lose my wife and family for good. Therefore, I willingly put on that suit and tie and I threw away the thug hat and mentality that went with the streets. I traded street life for the sincere dedication to a professional career. My day-to-day life consisted of sitting behind a desk and working with her in a credit repair company. Daily, I helped our customers break free from the debtor's prison as my mother-in-law helped to deliver me from my personal mental prison. Perhaps you're familiar with these areas of bondage, the kind that keep our minds locked up and limit our potential. I exchanged my street corner mentality—that was rooted in a fear of death and distrust for people—for a business mindset that offered our customers truth and a confident smile. My demeanor shifted, and I changed, as my mother-in-law empowered me and taught me how to empower others through credit.

My initial training in the credit business gave me a chance to earn thirty percent of the income from sales, and I learned to work hard for others as much as I could. The sky was my limit. I became a street hustler again, only this time I was seeking mortgage business clients and not drug customers. I sought out people who had poor credit and who had previously been denied for home loans. I had a friend, who was married to a doctor. They owned a mortgage company, and he sent me their rejected clients. With the training I was receiving, I was able to help many customers clean up their credit and purchase their first homes. I witnessed their lives change. These individuals began to accomplish their financial and life goals, and seeing this happen for them gave me hope for my future as well. Soon, I found myself teaching and counselling a variety of people on the value of having good credit. The potential in this industry and the people who needed help were countless. I never dreamed so many people suffered from debt. This was a different type of prison, but it was just as limiting, only in a different way. Helping people brought success my way. Things were popping off for me with my thirty percent sales commission.

I worked hard, learned more about the business, and soon I decided to go all the way in with the credit industry. I went to my mother-in-law and told her that I wanted to step out on my own. She said, "I pray you soar like an eagle."

With her blessing, I stepped out into the world of entrepreneurship. I became my own boss and ran the business my way using the skills she'd taught me. I had been in the credit business for about two years prior to starting my business. At this time, I had not won my wife all the way back, and we were still separated. I was proud of my accomplishments and I thought she would be too. Business grew and the company was doing so well that I had to hire people to help me. I trained several people, because the business grew so much that I could not handle all the clients. I understood the gift of advertising too, so I placed ads on some of the top radio stations in Charlotte to pull in clients. This made sense for me, because networking was always a part of my life, even from my earlier years. This was just like second nature to me, and I loved that I earned one hundred percent of the revenue now and not just thirty percent.

I enjoyed helping people, and the financial freedom gave me an opportunity to focus on my family as well as my business. Life was going so well, and it seemed too good to be true. I was approached by people from all walks of life, including the professionals, entertainers, athletes, you name it. I helped various people build their credit and my name and brand were growing in the credit industry.

Soon, I found out that the success *was indeed* too good to be true. In 2003, financial mistakes from my past came back to haunt me, and I had to return to prison for a short time a few years later after the trial proceedings were complete in 2008. Although this was a big blow to me, because I thought that things were all good, we continued to build during this entire ordeal. As a result, our family experienced a little normalcy despite the chaos of trial proceedings. My wife noticed my earnest efforts to succeed, and she and my family supported me through this difficult time. Instead of turning her back on me like many women do, we worked together to plan for our future. We purchased a house in 2005. She went to school to earn her real estate license in 2007. My legal troubles also inspired her to pursue a master's degree in business administration to help seal our future. This ordeal began in 2003, and in 2008, I was sentenced. I left to serve my thirty-month sentence on December 31 of that year. Although I would not have chosen this path for myself, I learned so much, and it made me a better man. I had made a decision to live right and take care of my family the honest way, yet another big mistake costed me precious time. Several people who have stuck with me throughout these ups and downs reach out to me all the time to thank me for changing their lives by continuing to press ahead despite the adversities. To know that my perseverance was an inspiration to others motivated me during my hard times. I have my wife to thank for much of my success, as well as me surviving these difficult years. We've been going strong for twenty-six years through the ups and downs.

I was locked away with multi-billionaire investment advisor Bernie Madoff; many people don't know his true story, despite what the media reported. In the prison gym, I worked out with men who shared their stories and 'schooled me about the system, just like a father would do his son. I learned so much hearing about their successes and setbacks with my own ears. I also served time with John Joseph Connolly Jr. a former FBI agent who was convicted of racketeering, obstruction of justice, and murder charges stemming from his relationship with James Whitey Bulger, Steve Flemmi, and the Irish Winter Hill Mafia. We walked the track together and became good friends. Preachers, teachers (all of us) make mistakes. People in law enforcement are not above the law. I am not writing about these men (or myself for that matter) for us to be judged; God will indeed judge us all righteously. I mentioned these points about my past to say that God can use the worst situations to teach us important life lessons that can bless others. Although I fell into the destructive cycle of the criminal justice system because I was trying to escape the system of poverty embedded within this country, it pushed me to dedicate myself to breaking that cycle. My experiences motivated me to learn as much as possible about how to help the average person break the chains, achieve financial freedom, and succeed in life.

Age has a way of teaching us to mature and share our lessons with others. These lessons are designed to help us win, because when we live, we learn, and my hope is that this book will help you become a winner in life. It's time to break the chains to the prisons of debt, poverty, and financial bondage. We don't have to become statistics and fall into the traps of our societies. This book will not only educate you, but also help you to educate the future generations of your family.

You can make a change for the better now, and I am dedicated to showing you how. Your prison may not have been physical like mine, but that doesn't mean that you aren't locked down. Mental prisons and chains lock people in bondage each day, because so many people are drowned in debt.

At the time of this writing, debt in America is at an all-time high, at $1.02 trillion, according to November 2017 Federal Reserve statistics. WalletHub.com reported that the average indebted household carries approximately $8,600 in outstanding credit card debt. An expert from WalletHub said that the last time the country's average household debt was that high was in the fourth quarter of 2007, right before the recession (that number was $8,400). I share these stats here to let you know that you are not alone if you have fallen into this trap, but to also encourage you that you can take control of this situation. You can break free.

I have mastered this "Prison of Debt" along with the school of hard knocks. I have prepared this book to empower you and your loved ones to conquer the debt that has put you in a mental prison of stress and despair. *Break the Chains* is different from your average credit book. I am being transparent with you to let you know that I have made significant mistakes, but I was not designed to stay in those places of lack.

Some of you reading this are just like me. You've made mistakes with your life and your finances, yet despite those things, you are called to be your own "Credit Guru." I didn't give myself that name, either. People in my life tell me daily how I have made an impact on their lives; these clients began calling me the "Credit Guru," which made me want to live up to that title. I want to impact your life as well. I want to help the single mothers, the young college students, the divorcees who have found themselves in debt, those who have been sick, without health insurance and as a result have accumulated tons of unpaid hospital bills that have ruined your credit; I want to speak to black males and let them know that they don't have to fall into the traps of the street.

I talk to my talented, beloved son every day. He thinks like I did as a young man. He is a music guru with his own mind, and I want him to apply healthy financial practices early. However, as a father, I've had to realize that you can lead a horse to water, but you can't make him drink. In addition to a son, I have three daughters; my oldest daughter just received her master's degree in psychology in May of 2018 and is ready for entrepreneurship. Our middle daughter works in health insurance and is an entrepreneur with an online children's boutique and specialty bakery shop. Our youngest daughter just graduated from college in May of 2018 with a degree in psychology as well. I call them diamonds in the rough… I believe you are a diamond in the rough, too. My book is especially written to all diamonds in the rough like you.

Take Control of the Chains to Break Them

Before we move on to the meat of this book and the specifics of how to (re)build your credit, I want to leave you with a few thoughts. The first is that you must take control of the chains that are holding you back in order to break them. In other words, become proactive about your credit situation. Do not sit around and hope that things get better. You purchased this book because you are tired of being in bondage. The only way to change your situation is to take control of your destiny, grab your chains, implement the important steps that we're going to discuss in this book, then break the chains through education and action. You can do it with this book, and if you need more help, I can work with you personally if you visit www.*malikdavis.com* or www.*yourcreditguru.net.* The purpose of this book is to teach you to believe in yourself and help you fix your credit. I realize some of you have busy lives and may not have the time to repair your credit on your own. My book will always be here for you when you are ready for the challenge. If not, reach out to me, and my company will do the work for you.

The rest of this book is designed to empower you with knowledge and education, tips, and secrets to improve your credit and establish important financial habits. Financial ignorance landed me behind bars, so I am big on teaching people the basics in order to create a strong foundation for success. I don't want what happened to me to be anyone else's story, especially not those of you who are reading this book. You don't have any more excuses, and now that you have this resource, pass it along to those you love.

I encourage you to read and take notes in every chapter, but if there is a topic that you want to focus on, revisit the **Table of Contents** and turn to the section that addresses what you need now.

Sit back and allow me to share with you how to become your own mastermind "Credit Guru!"

MALIK DAVIS

CHAPTER 2

What's the difference between a credit report and a credit score?

When most college students walk onto campus for the first week of school and orientation, they are bombarded with tons of information and some enticing offers. One of these offers is a shiny new plastic credit card promising financial freedom and safety in case of emergencies. This is the very type of situation that gets many people into years of financial bondage, thousands of dollars in debt, and bad credit. Many college students don't have jobs and they are just learning how to handle major responsibilities. Unfortunately, many students end up charging purchases which they cannot repay, or they miss payments (because of course they are more concerned with college life than finances), and they have bad credit before the end of freshman year. I've heard some stories where students have maxed out over ten credit cards by the time they've graduated college. Perhaps you are long past your college-age years, and if so, don't get too comfortable yet, because you're not off the hook. Adults make the same types of mistakes as our younger counterparts. Often we don't break the cycle of bad financial habits passed down through our bloodlines. Some of us just don't educate ourselves and gain access to our credit reports.

Have you ever applied for a bank loan? If so then you had to submit a credit application. This application allows lenders to access your credit report and credit scores to determine the likelihood of you repaying the loan for which you are applying. One point that shocks many people is that now even rental car agencies and employers often pull credit reports to determine if consumers can be trusted. Many people complain about their credit reports being pulled, but if you think about it, this protects companies who are defrauded by millions of dishonest consumers every year. I'm well aware that "things happen" that have affected the credit reports and scores of millions of people. Our goal is to get you above worry or anger when you learn that a company is pulling your credit.

Credit scores and reports are different. Let's make sure you know what those differences are since mastering these two items will help you break the chains and become your own Credit Guru. Credit reports include detailed information about your history of paying debts and obligations. That data in turn is calculated into a three-digit credit score that represents your credit worthiness. Let me break it down.

Credit reports provide a comprehensive list of your credit accounts and payment history, but they do not contain your credit score. In the United

States, there are three bureaus or companies that dominate the market. They are often referred to as "The Big Three." They are Equifax, Experian, and Transunion. The Big Three major credit bureaus compile information which details all the accounts you've ever opened or closed, the loans you've taken out, and how diligently you've paid off outstanding balances. Credit reports also contain public records such as judgements and bankruptcies. All of this information factors into your "credit history."

It is so important to establish a good credit history because lenders, landlords, insurers and employers all use credit reports to evaluate your borrowing history to decide whether you qualify for loans, credit cards, rental properties, you name it. If you are like most people, right about now, your mind is wondering *what does my credit report look like? What's on that thing?* Often, credit reports contain lots of information and many errors, which factors into their credit scores.

Many people never bother to correct the errors, not realizing that these errors can impact their credit scores which will affect the interest rates of loans or whether or not lenders will extend loans to them at all. Don't be one of those people; stay on top of your credit report and double-check yours now to see if the information is accurate.

THE BIG THREE CREDIT BUREAUS

CREDIT BUREAU	MAILING ADDRESS	PHONE NUMBER & WEBSITE	BETTER BUSINESS BUREAU RATING
Equifax	PO Box 740241 Atlanta, GA 30374	1-800-685-1111 www.equifax.com/	A
Transunion	PO Box 1000 Chester, PA 19022	1-800-916-8800 https://www.transunion.com/	A-
Experian	PO Box 2104 Allen, TX 75013	1-888-397-3742 http://www.experian.com/	B+

CREDIT GURU TIP:

You can pull free copies of your report at each individual company or from http://www.annualcreditreport.com. Your free credit report will not include your credit score.

CREDIT SCORE

Lenders use your credit score to evaluate how safe or how risky you are as a customer. Presently there are two types of scores, FICO Scores and VantageScore. Both FICO and VantageScore consider much of the same information, but they gather their data in different ways.

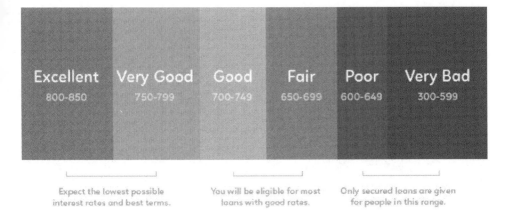

Excellent	Very Good	Good	Fair	Poor	Very Bad
800-850	750-799	700-749	650-699	600-649	300-599

Expect the lowest possible interest rates and best terms.

You will be eligible for most loans with good rates.

Only secured loans are given for people in this range.

What is the goal?

As you can see from the chart above, you want to aim to have a 750 credit score (or above) at all times until you can reach your highest potential. Here is how your credit scores are determined:

➢ How much money you owe compared to your credit limits; (credit utilization)

➢ How often you have applied for credit recently, called "hard inquiries"

➢ The types of credit you have, called a credit mix (can consist of fixed payments, like an auto loan, or variable payments, like a credit card).

Keep reading. The chart below explains how these scores are calculated.

Credit Scores

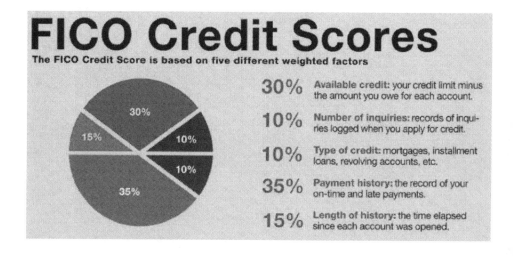

FICO Credit Scores
The FICO Credit Score is based on five different weighted factors

30% Available credit: your credit limit minus the amount you owe for each account.

10% Number of inquiries: records of inquiries logged when you apply for credit.

10% Type of credit: mortgages, installment loans, revolving accounts, etc.

35% Payment history: the record of your on-time and late payments.

15% Length of history: the time elapsed since each account was opened.

CHAPTER 3

Scoring Models

The two scoring models are FICO and VantageScore. Let's discuss FICO first. FICO stands for Fair, Isaac and Company; it is a data analytics company founded by Bill Fair and Earl Isaac in 1956 and it is one of two key players in the credit scoring industry. The FICO scoring model is based on credit reports from millions of consumers all at once. These reports are gathered from the three major credit bureaus. The reports are then analyzed with anonymous consumer data to generate an accurate scoring model. On the other hand, the Vantage scoring model uses a combined set of consumer files obtained from the three credit bureaus to come up with a single formula.*

Both FICO and VantageScore issue scores ranging from 300 to 850. In the past, VantageScore has used a range of 501 to 990. In 2017, VantageScore 4.0 was issued; the score range was adjusted with its 3.0 version released in 2013. VantageScore's numerical rankings now match FICO's.

*usatoday.com

Now it's easier and less complicated for us to check both FICO and VantageScore scores. To learn more about this score, visit **https://your.van-tagescore.com/interpret_scores.**

In general, credit scores will fluctuate based on your account activity. Credit scores of 690 and above are considered as "good" while 720 and above are considered "excellent." The two scoring models basically look at the same factors, so if you have a good score on one, you'll most likely have a good score on the other. It is important to note that you may have slightly different scores with each of the big three bureaus.

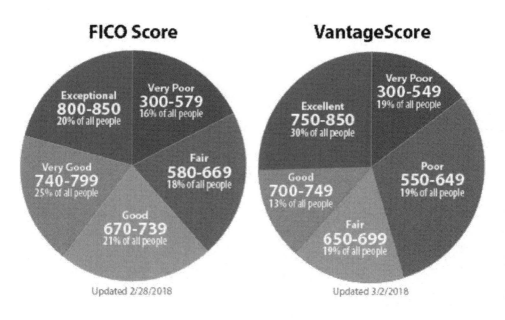

Source: badcredit.org

The Credit Score Range Scale

There are many different credit scores available to lenders, and they each develop their own credit score range. Why is that important? Because if you get your credit score, you need to know the credit score range you are looking at, so you understand where your number fits in. Here are the credit score ranges used by major credit scoring models:

➢ **FICO Score range: 300-850**

➢ **VantageScore 4.0 range: 300–850**

➢ **VantageScore scale (versions 1.0 and 2.0): 501–990**

➢ **Experian's PLUS Score: 330-830**

➢ **TransUnion New Account Score 2.0: 300-850**

➢ **Equifax Credit Score: 280–850**

A FICO score is the most commonly used score by potential lenders and credit card issuers. Lenders also use this score to determine your interest rate. The FICO scoring company uses a proprietary formula to measure your creditworthiness. Your credit reports from Equifax, Experian, and TransUnion are derived from data using this formula. The credit bureaus often will have slightly different data from one another, so your score will vary for each bureau.

Like I stated earlier, the FICO scoring model has been around for more than twenty-five years; however, to keep up with the current behavioral trends of consumers and meet the needs of lenders, The FICO score model has been redeveloped over the years. As a result, there are now multiple FICO score versions as well as "industry specific" versions that cater to auto and bankcard lenders.

At the time of me writing this, the latest version of FICO scores is the FICO score 9. This is what you call a Base FICO score. It is the most predictive score yet. Many lenders have already upgraded to the latest version. There are some differences that you should be mindful of and new factors that will impact your score:

➢ **Medical collections** are treated differently than other types of debt. Unpaid medical collections will have less of a negative impact on FICO Score 9.

➢ **Third-party collections** that have been paid off no longer have a negative impact.

➢ **Rental history**, when it's reported, it will factor into your score—this may be especially beneficial for people with a limited credit history.

This is great news to consumers with blemishes on their credit because it provides a bit more leniency.

What's the difference between base FICO Scores and industry-specific FICO Scores?

Base FICO scores are exactly how they sound. They are the starting point for your credit scores. Most companies will use this score, however there are certain organizations that have FICO scores specific to their industries. Base FICO Scores were created to predict the likelihood of a consumer not paying as agreed in the future on a credit obligation, whether it's a credit card, student loan, mortgage or other credit product. Industry-specific FICO scores are important for specific industries such as credit card or automobile, and they also assess the likelihood of a consumer not paying as agreed on a specific type of credit obligation.

Industry-specific FICO Scores incorporate the predictive power of base FICO Scores, and at the same time, provide lenders a further-refined way to measure; this is tailored to the type of credit the consumer is seeking.

There are a variety of common features with FICO Auto Scores and FICO Bankcard Scores. Individual lenders determine which is most relevant to their credit review processes. Remember that industry-specific scores range from 250-900, while the base FICO ranges from 300-850. Therefore, a lot of times you can apply for the same type of loan at two different places and end up with different scores. It just depends on the lender.

Which Version of the FICO Score is important to you?

If you want to get a car, it will be beneficial to know your FICO Auto Score. In the case of credit cards, you want to pay attention to your FICO Bankcard Score. Base FICO scores are the most common and these will be important to you if you want to buy a home.

If you want to know a FICO Industry score, sign up for FICO Score Open Access Program. The program will provide you with the industry FICO scores that lenders use to access your account, and they work with over 100 financial institutions. FICO Score Open Access for Credit and Financial Counseling enables credit and financial counseling providers to share FICO Scores with their customers like you.

Let's look at another popular scoring model now.

VantageScore Model

TransUnion, Equifax, and Experian joined forces in 2006 to create a new type of credit score: VantageScore. It was designed to compete with the FICO Score created by Fair Isaac Corporation. The VantageScore model considers common data including on-time payments, low credit card balances, new credit obligations, bank accounts, and other assets to calculate its score. The VantageScore 3.0 release needs only one month of credit history to establish a score, as opposed to the six months needed for FICO and other models. VantageScore has some other unique attributes; it ignores collections —paid or unpaid — (under $250), and provides special treatment of victims of a natural disaster. According to its website, with the VantageScore 3.0 and 4.0 models, only payment history information that would negatively impact a consumer's credit score is "set to neutral" so consumers are not impacted if they are not able to pay their bills after a natural disaster. VantageScore also excludes paid medical collections. The VantageScore uses information from all three credit bureaus, but weighs certain factors more heavily or less heavily than the FICO algorithm. Your scores for both FICO and VantageScore should be similar, but rarely identical.

CHAPTER 4

What is the FCRA and what is it intended to do?

Like anything in life there are forces that you cannot see dictating your success. In the world of credit, these "forces" are the credit bureaus and an important law known as FCRA. You may be thinking, well why do I need to know about FCRA? It's important to start here, at the basics, so that you know the laws governing your credit outlook and how the big companies interact with you and do things to impact your wallet.

You have rights as a consumer, and this chapter is going to help you understand them better. Before we get into what you need to know about the FCRA, let's quickly recap. If you've been following along, you now know the credit score range (300-900); your goal in order to reach an "excellent credit score" is 750. We've discussed the various credit scoring models and the difference between Base FICO and Industry-specific scores.

As with every great American institution, the credit industry also has a governing body with rules and regulations that are designed to keep consumers safe. The Fair Credit Reporting Act (FCRA) is a federal law that regulates credit reporting agencies and compels them to ensure the information they gather and distribute is a fair and accurate summary of a consumer's credit history. The law is intended to protect consumers from misinformation being used against them. This is good news for you. Continue reading why! You've entered my world of all things CREDIT, and are well on your way to becoming your own Credit Guru. The information within this chapter includes some helpful facts about FCRA and your rights that I've gathered from Debt.org and other sources.

I recommend taking out your highlighter, and as you read this financial manual, mark the information that is foreign to you.

I just told you that the FCRA is good news for you. The reason why is that the FCRA's main priority is to guide and oversee the way credit reporting agencies use the information they receive regarding your credit history. The law is intended to protect consumers from misinformation being used against them. It offers very specific guidelines about how credit reporting agencies collect and verify information and outlines reasons that information can be released.

History of FCRA

The law was passed in 1970 and amended twice. It is primarily aimed at the three major credit reporting agencies — Experian, Equifax and

WHAT IS THE FCRA?

TransUnion — because of the widespread use of the information those bureaus collect and sell. The law also applies to banks, credit unions, and agencies that sell medical records and check writing or rental history records, as well as any business that uses information on credit reports for hiring purposes. According to debt.org, the FCRA has come up often in media reports because advocacy groups question the accuracy of the information credit reporting agencies gather and consumers' ability to dispute that information and have it removed from their credit report. The questions raised regarding the credit bureaus help you out as a consumer. Now, they are required to investigate disputes. So feel empowered to take an active role in what is on your credit report. Review it regularly and dispute what doesn't look right. Learn more about your rights later in the chapter.

FCRA and Credit Reporting Agencies

Credit reporting agencies (CRA), which we will discuss A LOT in this book, are responsible for gathering, processing and archiving credit information on consumers.

According to recent data, the CRAs have information on more than 200 million Americans. They sell that information to help businesses make decisions about granting loans or credit. They sell that information to help businesses make decisions about granting loans or credit. In a 2017 Inc.com article, Brett Horn, an industry analyst with Morningstar is quoted, "It's a pretty simple business model, actually. They [credit bureaus] gather as much information about you from lenders, aggregate it, and sell it back to them." It may not seem fair, but the law allows this.

The agencies collect information on every consumer's use of credit and their bill-paying habits. The data comes from "information suppliers," or any business that extends credit to customers. They also gather information from public records like court judgments and bankruptcy filings. Information suppliers transmit consumer credit information electronically to the credit reporting agencies on a continuous basis; this is why credit reports could change almost daily, depending on the level of a consumer's activity.

The CRAs feed the data they receive into their own set of algorithms to come up with a score that predicts a consumer's creditworthiness. CRAs do not make decisions on whether consumers get loans. That decision is made by banks, credit unions, mortgage companies or other companies that extend credit. The information from the CRA is used to set the interest rate and conditions for a loan.

CREDIT GURU TIP:

With this information, be aware of who you give your information to. Keep your credit applications and open accounts to a minimum. Realize that when you change your address, become involved in a lawsuit, file bankruptcy, or file taxes, etc., all of this information becomes available on your credit report.

You have rights.

You have rights pertaining to your credit data and how companies handle it. There are do's and don'ts that lenders and other companies with access to your financial history must follow. Being educated on your rights will truly pay off for you when you begin to repair and build credit. With this list of rights, you have more facts to include in dispute letters to compel companies to remove data that cannot be verified. The FCRA provides a list of consumer rights regarding individuals' credit history information. Bookmark this page so that as you come across questionable data in regards to your credit, you can refer to these rights and dispute the information if necessary.

The Federal Fair Credit Reporting Act (FCRA) promotes the accuracy, fairness, and privacy of information in the files of consumer reporting agencies. There are many types of consumer reporting agencies, including credit bureaus and specialty agencies (such as agencies that sell information about check writing histories, medical records, and rental history records). Here is a summary of your major rights under the FCRA.

Under the Fair Credit Reporting Act, you have a right to:

- **Access to Your Credit Report** – The act requires credit reporting agencies to provide you with any information in your credit file upon request once a year. You must have proper identification. You have a right to a free copy of your credit report within 15 days of your request.

- **Protected Access** – The act limits access to your file to those with a valid need. That would usually be banks, insurance companies, employers, landlords or others doing business that involves offering credit. You also have the right to know who has requested your credit report in the last year or, for employment-related requests, two years.

- **Accurate Reporting** – If inaccurate information is discovered in your file, the consumer reporting agency must examine the disputed information, usually within 30 days. If the inaccurate information cannot be verified, the consumer reporting agency has a responsibility to remove it. If you are not able to clear up the matter, you are allowed to add a statement to your credit file explaining the situation.

- **Have Outdated Information Removed** – Negative information must be removed from your file after seven years. Bankruptcy, however, may remain on record for 10 years, and criminal record information can remain indefinitely.

- **Maintain Medical Information Privacy** – You are protected from having medical information in a consumer report, as creditors are prohibited from obtaining or using medical information when making a credit decision.

- **Limit Unsolicited Credit Offers** – The law allows you to request to have your name and address removed from unsolicited prescreened offer lists for credit and insurance. To opt out of such correspondence, call (888) 5-OPTOUT (888-567-8688).

- **Protect Your Personal Account Numbers** – Businesses are not permitted to publish full credit card numbers on receipts. The law also allows you to protect your Social Security number by having it truncated on your credit report.

- **Receive Notification of Possible Negative Information** – You have the right to be notified if any financial institution submits, or plans to submit, negative information to a credit reporting agency. This information may be included in a billing statement or a notice of default.

- **Seek Damages** – You have the right to sue and seek damages in a state or federal court from anyone, such as a consumer reporting agency or a user of consumer reports, who violates the Fair Credit Reporting Act.

- **Know When Your Credit Report Is Used Against You** – If you are denied credit, insurance or employment because of your credit report, you can ask for the specific reason for the denial.

- **Know Your Credit Scores** – You have a unique credit score with each credit bureau, which you can request. In some cases, you may be required to pay for this information.

Source: Debt.org

CREDIT GURU TIP:

For more information, including additional rights, go to www.ftc.gov/credit or write to Consumer Response Center, Room 130-A, Federal Trade Commission, 600 Pennsylvania Ave. N.W., Washington, D.C. 20580

CHAPTER 5

Credit Repair Overview

OK now that you know what's what in the world of credit, it's time to figure out how to fix bad credit (if it applies). **Chapter 8 also has detailed steps to repair your credit, but this is an overview.** If your credit is holding you back, pursue credit repair aggressively. It's your right as a consumer, and it's also an obligation that you have to yourself—for your future. Who wants to live with bad credit? It makes your life more difficult and definitely more expensive. These days most, if not all, companies charge higher interest rates to people with bad credit. This practice contributes to the system of helping the rich get richer while the poor get poorer. Insurance companies often charge drivers with poor credit higher rates. Utility and even cell phone companies will now check your credit to decide whether you should pay a security deposit. We all know that banks check credit scores before they issue credit cards, and employers consider credit prior to hiring for certain positions. As years go by, the list of companies who check your credit will probably grow instead of decrease. This will hinder you today and tomorrow and affect your potential to secure a loan and make big purchases. The discussion below will help you repair your credit and avoid bad credit altogether.

Why Pursue Credit Repair?

Credit repair is critical to saving money on insurance, loans, and credit cards, but that's not the only reason to repair your credit. If you dream of starting your own business or just want the security of knowing you can borrow money when you want to, you should repair your credit sooner rather than later.

Credit Repair and Bankruptcies

Many people give up on their credit after filing for bankruptcy, but this is when you should become more determined to have good credit. Bankruptcy, while it is not the best situation to be in, can be the reset you need to truly focus on your finances. It stays on your credit reports for ten years. Ten years is not forever, and so while that bankruptcy (or other negative marks) still contributes to your credit score in a negative way, repair by rebuilding good credit to establish a better financial outlook. Bankruptcies hinder your progress in restoring financial stability. So if you can avoid it, do so at all costs.

Credit Repair Because of Errors

On average, one in five Americans report an error on their reports. This is a major reason to pursue credit repair. There is a high chance that there is something incorrect on your report. One even better reason is that it's much easier than people think to get errors and erroneous information removed. Most people have errors and items that cannot be proved on their credit reports and those items don't have to be there. Are you a person with a bad credit score because you haven't taken the time to pay attention to your credit report? Here are some questions to ask yourself regarding your credit report:

- Is all the personal information correct?
- Is the work history correct?
- Is your name spelled correctly?
- Is the length of open accounts mentioned correctly?
- Are there items in collections that are unfamiliar?
- Are there any additional errors on your credit report?

Take the time to review your credit report to ensure that the name, addresses, employers, and accounts opened and closed belong to you. When you notice inaccuracies, dispute them.

By pursuing credit repair, you can:

• **Get rid of erroneous, outdated information**: Negative records should not remain on your credit report indefinitely. There are laws that have been in to place for the CRAs to remove negative information after a certain period (see the chart below). They may not always follow the credit law and you may have to take the lead in identifying and disputing old data.

• **Remove debts that have been discharged in bankruptcy**: Your debt-to-income ratio weighs heavily on your overall credit score. If your credit report reflects debts that no longer exist, your credit score may suffer unnecessarily.

CREDIT REPAIR OVERVIEW

HOW LONG DOES NEGATIVE INFORMATION REMAIN ON A CREDIT REPORT?

TYPE OF NEGATIVE INFORMATION	LENGTH OF TIME REMAINS ON CREDIT REPORT
Lawsuits and Judgments	7 years
Tax Liens (paid/released)	7 years from payment
Tax liens (unpaid)	Indefinitely
Charge off Profit and Loss	7 years
Late payments	7 years
Debt collections	7 years
Bankruptcy	10 years
Other adverse information	7 years
Inquiries	2 years (affects credit score for only the first 12 months)

Often, when I counsel my clients on the financial behavior that has led to their poor credit scores, they are often surprised by something that they learn. The next chapter goes into more detail about the negative information that affects your credit score. Sulk in this information so that you don't repeat any of the mistakes you made in the past. Can you feel those chains breaking yet??? I CAN!

CHAPTER 6

Factors Leading to Poor Credit

As flawed individuals, there is not just one reason why people have bad credit. Usually, we have made a series of poor decisions to affect our credit or have not established credit at all: both scenarios lead to negative scores. You might be tempted to skip pass this section so that you can figure out how to repair your credit, but I caution you against that. One major key to breaking the chains of financial bondage and bad credit is to change your mindset, which will then help you change your behavior. This section is going to take you to school, make you aware of the mistakes that you have made in the past, and help you figure out why it's been a challenge for you to improve your credit score.

Here are some of the factors that have a negative impact on your credit score:

Late payments

Did you know that thirty-five percent of your credit score is your payment history? If you are consistently late on your credit card payments, this will only hurt your credit score. Pay your credit card, auto payments, rent/mortgage bills on time to preserve your credit score. Creditors may report your activity to credit bureaus once every thirty days.

Not Paying at All

Have you ever been in a financial strain and were tempted to skip paying important bills? Completely ignoring your bills is a huge mistake and is much worse than paying late. Each month you miss a payment, you're one month closer to having the account charged off. In addition, not paying important bills like your car note or mortgage can lead to bigger financial and credit problems, including repossessions and foreclosures. Don't miss your payments; if you are struggling, call and ask for an extension or make other arrangements with your creditors.

Charge-offs

If creditors think you are not going to pay your balances, they will charge-off your accounts. This account status is one of the worst factors to affect your credit score. It means you've been delinquent in paying your bill(s), which does not look good with future creditors. It's basically like someone saying, "We might as well forget about getting our money back from this person! This is a useless cause." Don't be a useless cause.

Collections

Creditors might send your account to collections before or after charging it off. This is when the original company that you owed has sold your account to a collections agency. A collection status shows that the creditor gave up trying to get payment from you and hired someone else to do it. When this happens, the higher your score, the more points your credit score will drop. Many credit card accounts are sent to a collection agency after 180 days of non-payment. Either the original creditor or the collection agency may report the account in collections to a credit bureau, and they do not have to inform you when this happens.

Defaults

When you do not satisfy your end of the loan contract, you default. Defaulting on a loan is comparable to having a charge off. It's generally a bad practice to default on loans. In personal/human terms, this is what would happen if you lent a friend money and they refused to pay or ignored the deal they made with you to get the loan.

Bankruptcy

Filing for bankruptcy will damage your credit score. A bankruptcy will stay on your credit report for ten years, making it difficult to reestablish credit or apply for major purchases that require loans. I always recommend seeking other alternatives such as consumer credit counseling before filing for bankruptcy. Often times, creditors and debt collectors will be willing to make arrangements that will require a lesser payment amount than you owe. Creditors will often create these types of arrangements with consumers prior to bankruptcy because afterwards, they will not receive any payments at all. Exhaust all of your options first, before filing for bankruptcy.

Foreclosure

Once you miss two to four mortgage payments, generally banks start the foreclosure process. Remember, creditors report your account status to the credit reporting agencies every thirty days or so. When you get behind on your payments, your account will become delinquent, your credit score will lower, and it will be difficult to secure mortgage loans in the future.

Judgments

When you receive a judgment, it means that you completely dodged paying your bills and the court had to get involved to make you pay your debt. Both paid and unpaid judgments hurt your credit score, but it is better to have a paid judgment. Often, consumers fail to realize that certain legal activity is reported to the credit bureaus. If it relates to your finances, chances are, it will also end up on your credit report.

High Credit Card Balances

The second most critical part of your credit score is your level of debt. Debt level is measured by your credit utilization (there is an entire chapter on this). When you have high credit card balances, as it relates to your credit limit, your credit utilization rate is higher; this decreases your credit score.

Maxed out Credit Cards

Refrain from maxing out your credit cards. This is a sure fire way to see a drop in your credit score. Maxed out and over-the-limit credit card balances make your credit utilization 100 percent or more. This is damaging for your credit score. In general, a good credit utilization ratio should be less than thirty percent. That means you're using less than thirty percent of the total credit available to you. To achieve thirty percent credit utilization, you should keep your balances below thirty percent of the credit limit. For example, on a credit card with a $1,000 limit, you should keep your balance below $300.

Closing Credit Cards with Balances

You should never close credit cards that have balances. When you close a credit card that still has a balance, your credit limit drops to $0 while your balance remains. This makes it look like you've maxed out your credit card, causing your score to drop.

Closing Old Credit Cards

Most people think it's a good idea to close old credit cards after they've paid off the balances, but it can actually have a negative effect. This is because your credit history accounts for fifteen percent of your score. Having a longer credit history is better. Closing old credit cards, especially your oldest card, makes your credit history seem shorter than it really is. I've seen situations where old, negative items have dropped off of people's credit reports after seven years, and the only items remaining are closed credit cards. Their scores remain low because they lack credit history.

Closing Cards with Available Credit

The lower your credit utilization, the higher your credit score. If you have credit cards with a zero balance and available credit, do NOT close them. This will hurt your credit utilization. It's best to keep your cards open, even if you're not using them. The more cards you have with very low (to zero) credit utilization, the higher your score will be.

New Credit

New credit accounts for ten percent of your credit score. If you are applying for new lines of credit, you may see a minimum drop in your score. According to MyFico.com, if you apply for several new credit cards within a short period of time, multiple requests for your credit report information (inquiries) will appear on your report. Shopping for new credit can equate with higher risk, but most credit scores are not affected by multiple inquiries from auto or mortgage lenders within a short period of time. Typically, these are treated as a single inquiry and will have little impact on the credit score. (The next chapter has more information about credit inquiries.)

Mix it Up

You want to mix up the type of credit that you have. The variety of accounts you have actually accounts for ten percent of your score. You never want to be in a situation where you have only one type of credit, such as only student loans, credit cards or just one auto loan. This will become a factor for you when you don't have a substantial amount of credit information in your credit history. You should have a good mixture of revolving credit.

CREDIT GURU TIP:

Improve your score and save on interest. The chart below shows how to see how negative factors could affect your credit FICO scores.

DAMAGE POINTS: How certain factors affect FICO scores		
Credit Factor	If your score is 680	If your score is 780
Maxed-out Credit Card	Down 10 to 30 points	Down 25 to 45 points
30/day Late payment	Down 60 to 80 points	Down 90 to 110 points
Debt settlement	Down 45 to 60 points	Down 105 to 125 points
Foreclosure	Down 85 to 105 points	Down 140 to 160 points
Bankruptcy	Down 130 to 150 points	Down 220 to 240 points

Source: FICO

POOR SCORES

30-Year fixed rate with a Principal Loan Amount of $250,000			
FICO SCORE	**APR**	**MONTHLY PAYMENT**	**INTEREST PAID**
Above 720	5.71%	$1,453	$272,928
620-719	5.76% to 7.84%	$1,466 to $1,807	$277,845 to $400,381
Below 620	8.452% to 9.234%	$1,914 to $2,054	$438,957 to $489,365

Source: Credit Resource Corp

Above is a scenario of the type of interest one would pay on a home loan of $250,000. Poor credit really costs you in the long run. A person with poor credit could ultimately pay approximately $216,437 more on the same exact home loan as a person with good credit. So, your neighbor (with good credit) and you (with poor credit) could have the same type of home with the same loan amount, but your neighbor will only pay $1,453 a month for their mortgage while you will you're paying $2,054 for the same mortgage. That's a difference of $601 per month that you could use towards other household obligations. Do you see why credit repair is important?

CREDIT GURU TIP:

Focus on a few of the factors in this chapter each quarter. As you improve your behavior and activity in these areas, you will improve your credit score.

CHAPTER 7

What You Need to Know About Credit Inquiries

If you're like many of us, you've looked at your credit report at some point and thought, *why are all these companies pulling my credit report*?! While some "soft inquiries" are permitted by law, in general, companies should not access your credit report under false pretenses. When this happens, these creditors are in violation of Federal law. You may be able to sue a company that violates your rights.

The Fair Credit Reporting Act (FCRA) requires a business to have an acceptable reason for accessing your credit report. These acceptable reasons include:

- Some government agencies might check your credit report before issuing certain licenses
- Valid business transactions
- Insurance underwriting: some insurance providers use your credit score to assess the likelihood of you filling a claim.

- To grant credit: if you've applied for a credit card, loan, or other credit-based services, the business has permission to access your credit report to determine whether you qualify. (When this happens, you are also entitled to a free copy of your credit report).
- Debt collection: debt collectors can use your credit report to obtain information, (such as your address or place of employment,) that would help them collect a debt.
- Employment: current and potential employers may check your credit report before hiring you for certain positions, particularly financial and upper-level management positions.

There are two types of credit inquiries (hard inquiries and soft inquiries). You may have both types of inquiries on your credit report, but you only need to concern yourself with the hard inquiries. Inquiries that are made because of an application you made for credit are the ones that affect your score. They are considered "hard" or voluntary inquiries.

You may have reviewed your credit report and noticed several inquiries that appear to be from businesses you did not seek out for credit. These are companies who usually check your credit to offer you pre-approved credit card or loan offers. You may have also noticed inquiries from potential employers or companies with whom you already have established relationships. These are all soft inquiries and do not count against your credit.

WHAT YOU NEED TO KNOW ABOUT CREDIT INQUIRIES

How Inquiries Affect Your Score

Companies gauge the risk that you may default on new credit obligations by the number of inquiries you have on your credit report. When a consumer has too many inquiries, it may appear he or she is taking on too much debt or that the person is in financial trouble and are looking for credit to climb out of it. Having numerous inquiries can reduce your credit score.

Inquiries will remain on your credit report for two years. Only those (hard) inquiries made within the last year are included in your credit score calculation. The most recent inquiries have the most impact on your score.

Inquiries and Rate Shopping

When you shop around for a mortgage or auto loan, you want to get the best rate possible. Some people may worry that having your credit checked by several lenders could hurt your credit score. You can rest assured that most credit score calculations treat all mortgage and auto inquiries as a single inquiry, as long as the inquiries are made within a certain period of time. For the latest version of the FICO score, this period is forty-five days.

CREDIT GURU TIP:

Be very selective whom you allow to pull your credit. If you know you will be in the market for a new vehicle or other items that will require new lines of credit, plan accordingly. Determine when you will go rate shopping, and make it happen all within one month to be on the safe side.

CHAPTER 8

Credit Repair Tips

Until you can live on cash alone, credit will be crucial for you in today's fast-paced society. Most of us use credit almost every day without even thinking about it: credit cards, car payments, house payments, etc. Unfortunately, many people pay no attention to "credit repair" until they've been denied for a loan, apartment, or receive an extremely high interest rate because of their credit. A poor credit rating affects far more than your ability to get a loan: you will also have problems obtaining any kind of credit at all (credit cards, utilities, etc.). In addition, with poor credit, you could be required to pay deposits on phone lines and utilities, and you will face problems with renting property. It's very important to take steps to repair your credit as quickly as possible.

Here are a variety of tips to help you begin repairing your credit today. You may need to implement some or all of these tips. The key is to prioritize them by what makes the most sense for your situation.

1. Order the latest copies of your credit report.

This step is crucial. All credit information is reported by banks and lenders to credit bureaus, who in turn hold the key to credit repair. Most people never consider obtaining their credit reports until they are attempting credit repair, but it's always to set up a credit monitoring system to monitor your credit often. You can always visit my website www.yourcreditguru.net for more information and to sign up for my credit monitoring product and receive all three credit bureau reports and scores for the price of $29.99. You can also visit my Instagram page @malikdavis211 and click on the link in my bio to get started. The benefit of credit monitoring is that you will know when something changes on your report. With the prevalence of identity theft, this is a beneficial investment. According to a 2018 poll by The Harris Poll, nearly 60 million Americans have been affected by identity theft. You want to know when something changes on your credit report, and you want to know it immediately so that you can stop fraud and clear up any inaccuracies that could affect your financial future. Before you can start repairing your credit, you must know what you need to repair. Your credit report contains all the mistakes you've made that have led to poor credit. Read through your credit report to see the negative items affecting your credit score.

Why order all three reports?

Some creditors and lenders that you work with might report only to one of the three credit bureaus. In addition, you may have disputed an item on one report that was removed yet is still showing on the other reports. Ordering all three reports will give you a complete view of your credit history and enable you to repair your credit at all three bureaus instead of just one. Some people delay ordering their credit reports and starting the repair process, because it seems like a daunting task. I want to assure you that no matter how bad your credit appears to be; it can be repaired. Updated credit reports will empower you to begin the process of change. You want the total picture, which is why you order all three.

It's a good idea to make an extra copy of each report in case you need to dispute information. You can send the copy of your report to the credit bureaus and keep a copy for yourself.

Another option would be to request a free credit report (I do not recommend this because you will only receive one report without scores). By law, you are entitled to free credit reports from each of the three credit bureaus each year. This yearly free credit report is available through AnnualCreditReport.com.

Additional ways to get your credit report for free

Here is a credit hack. if you are turned down for a credit card or loan, the company must provide you with a notice that includes the credit bureau

87

that reported you as having poor credit, and you can then request a report from this bureau. You're also entitled to a free credit report if you're currently receiving government assistance, if you're unemployed and planning to look for a job soon, or if you think you've been a victim of credit card fraud or identity theft. In these cases, order your free credit reports directly from the credit bureaus.

2. **Review your reports for errors.**

Once you have obtained your credit reports, read through them completely. I'll mention this again, but you want to have your highlighter available to note which accounts you plan on disputing. Your credit report may be several pages long if you have a long credit history. Trying to read and understand your credit report may be a bit overwhelming and a lot to digest especially if this is your first time reviewing a credit report. Take your time and read carefully.

➤ Familiarize yourself with your credit reports. The reports from each bureau will look similar. If you want one that is easier to read, you can order a tri-merge report, such as the one that I offer at www.yourcreditguru.net. Each credit report contains your personal identifying information, detailed history for each of your accounts, any items that have been listed in the public record like a bankruptcy, and the inquiries that have been made to your credit report.

How do you decide what needs to be repaired?

➢ Incorrect information, including accounts that aren't yours, payments that have been incorrectly reported as late, etc.

➢ Past due accounts that are late, charged off, or have been sent to collections

➢ Maxed out accounts that are over the credit limit

I suggest that you use several different color highlighters to mark your reports for repair. You'll take a different approach for incorrect information than you would for a past due account so using different colors will save time when you are re-reading your credit reports.

3.   Dispute credit errors.

Did you know that as a consumer, you have the right to dispute any information in your credit report that is inaccurate, incomplete, or you believe cannot be verified? Let me repeat that last one: if you believe an item on your report cannot be verified, especially if it is in collections, dispute it. Many creditors send consumer accounts to collections agencies without all of the information necessary to identify the consumer. When these accounts are investigated, they are often removed. So therefore, even if an account belongs to you, if it is in collections, I would dispute it if I were you, or you can hire me to do it for you. **(That was a bonus Credit Tip.)**

When you order your credit reports, you'll receive instructions on how to dispute errors. Credit reports ordered online typically come with instructions for making disputes online, but you can also make disputes over the phone and through the (snail) mail.

Best methods for disputing inaccurate negative information:

It's often quicker and easier to dispute credit errors online, and this is also true for disputes you make over the phone. However, sending your disputes through regular mail has several advantages. First, you can also send proof that supports your dispute, such as receipts proving that you paid(s) for your records. You can also keep a copy of the dispute letter(s) for your records, and if you send your dispute via certified mail with return receipt requested (which you should), you have proof of the time you mailed it out. This is important because credit bureaus have thirty to forty-five days to investigate and respond to your dispute(s).

Since you'll be sending multiple disputes, you can keep a credit report dispute template on your computer that you can modify for different disputes and different credit bureaus. There is an entire section toward the end of this book with several dispute templates.

Sending your Dispute

When you send your dispute to the credit bureaus, you should also include a copy of your credit report, a photo ID, a copy of your social security card, and a copy of a utility bill with your current address and any other supporting documents. Only send copies (not the original) of your credit report and make sure that you have highlighted the accounts or information that you're disputing. If you do not wish to send in a hard copy of your credit report, you can list the accounts along with the account numbers that you wish to dispute in your dispute letter. If you don't send enough information about your dispute, the credit bureau can decide your dispute is frivolous and decline to investigate the dispute or update your credit report. If your dispute is legitimate, the credit bureau will conduct an investigation and send you a response through the mail. Normally, they will send a response within thirty days.

Credit Companies Dispute Alternative

You can also send your disputes directly to the creditor or business that listed the information on your credit report. They have the same legal obligation to investigate your dispute and remove inaccurate, incomplete, **or unverifiable information from your credit report. I recommend beginning with the credit bureaus, since they control the reports and the scores, and if the disputes are not decided in your favor, you can reach out to the companies directly.**

What happens after a dispute?

If the dispute is successful and your credit report is updated, the bureau will make the change, (sometimes) alert the other credit bureaus, and send you an updated copy of your credit report. To the contrary, if the item

91

isn't removed from your credit report, your report will be updated to show that you've disputed the information and you'll be given the opportunity to add a personal statement to your credit report. Personal statements don't affect your credit score, but they give additional insight into your dispute when a business manually reviews your credit report.

4.   Tackle past-due accounts.

Your goal is to have all your past due accounts reported as "current" or at least "paid." As I stated earlier in the book, your payment history impacts thirty-five percent of your credit score. Since payment history is such a large part of your credit score, having several past due accounts on your credit report will significantly hurt your score. Taking care of these issues are crucial to repairing your credit.

Get your past due accounts to a "current" status before they become labeled as charge offs. A charge-off is one of the worst account statuses on your credit report and it happens once your payment is 180 days past due.

If you pay the total amount due on a delinquent account (less than 180 days past due) you can prevent it from becoming a charge-off. Please be aware, the further behind you are, the higher your payments will be, and the bigger the mountain you will have to climb to get caught up. Contact your creditor soon to figure out what you can do to make your accounts current. They may be willing to waive some of the late penalties or spread the past due balance over a few payments. Let each creditor know that you want to avoid having a charge-off but need some help. They may even be willing to re-age your account to show your payments as current rather than delinquent, but you'll have to actually talk to your creditors to negotiate. When your account is "re-aged" it means that you've worked out an arrangement with a creditor, who has agreed to take the account out of delinquent status and stop reporting the delinquency to the credit bureaus.

5.   Handle charge-offs.

You're still responsible for charged-off balances. As charge-offs get older they have less of an impact, however, the outstanding balance(s) will make it hard (sometimes impossible) to get approved for new credit and loans. Part of your credit repair must include paying charge-offs or having them removed. If you pay a charge-off in full, your credit report will be updated to show a zero account balance, meaning the account is paid. The charge-off status will continue to be reported for seven years from the date of the charge off. Another option is to settle charge-offs for less than the original balance. If the creditor agrees to accept a settlement and cancel the rest of the debt, the settlement status will go on your credit report and stay on for seven years. You may be able to convince the creditor to delete the "charge-off" status in exchange for payment, but this isn't easily done. It's important to pay your charge-off OR dispute them. If you can get a favorable account status—that's an added bonus.

6. Take care of your collection accounts.

Past due accounts get sent to a collection agency after they've been charged-off or have fallen behind several months. Even accounts that aren't normally listed on your credit report can be sent to a collection agency and added to your credit, such as a cell phone or utility bill (if you do not pay them).

Your approach to paying collections will be much like that for charge-offs. You can pay the debts in full and even try to get the debt erased from your credit report once you do (called pay-for-delete). Another option is to settle the account for less than the balance due. The collection will stay on your credit report for seven years based on the original delinquency. As I mentioned earlier in the book, sometimes, companies are willing to negotiate accounts that are charged-off or in collections, since often, they will not receive any payment on these accounts otherwise.

7. Bring high account balances below your limit.

Credit utilization is a ratio that compares your total debt to total credit. This is another big chunk of the credit score pie. It accounts for thirty percent of your score. The higher your balances, the more it hurts your credit score. Bring maxed out credit cards below the credit limit, then work to pay the balances off completely. To have the best possible credit score, keep your balances at less than thirty percent of the credit limit, however, ten percent is best.

CREDIT GURU TIP:

If it will take you some time to get these balances below the limit, you want to make sure that you pay a little more than the minimum amount due each month in the meantime.

How Loan Balances affect Your Credit Score

Your loan balances or installment accounts also affect your credit score in a similar way as revolving accounts. The credit score calculation compares your current loan balance to the original loan amount. The closer your loan balances are to the original amount you borrowed, the more it hurts your credit score. Focus first on paying down credit card balances because they have more impact on your credit score.

Strategy: Past Due Accounts verses High Balances

You should prioritize where you spend your money. If you have high balances and past due balances, prioritize accounts that are in danger of becoming past due. Get as many of these accounts current as possible, preferably all of them. Then, work on bringing down your credit card balances. Next focus on the accounts that have already been charged-off or sent to a collection agency.

8. Get new credit.

OK lift your head. We've worked through most of the hard stuff. Now, it's time to rebuild. After you've resolved the negative items on your credit report, work on adding positive information. Payments made on time help your score. Maintain the credit cards and loans that you have on time.

You might have to reestablish your credit by opening a new account(s). Past delinquencies can keep you from getting approved for a major credit card so limit your credit card applications to one, at the most, two, until your credit score improves. This will keep your credit inquiries low. Credit inquiries are added to your credit report each time you make a new application for credit and too many of them hurts your credit score and your ability to get approved.

If you get denied for a major credit card, try applying for a secured credit card. If you have bad credit and you've been denied for credit in the past, skip applying for major credit cards and open a secured account instead. You can open a secured credit card by adding $200 or more to an account. As you visit different online credit companies or search online for information about credit, you may start receiving ads for new credit cards and some of them may be secured cards. It may be a good idea to avoid these offers and go to your bank or credit union instead for a card so that you are establishing credit while you build your relationship with your financial institution. This will help you in the future if you want to secure additional financial products. When you open the account, you will "secure" your balance with a specific amount to open it. As you charge items and pay down your balance each month on your new secured card, your credit score will increase. While you are using your own funds to build your credit, it's a helpful strategy.

Another way to improve your credit is to become an authorized user on a family member or friend's credit card ONLY after your credit has been cleaned up or repaired. It would be pointless to become an authorized user if your credit is still poor.

CREDIT GURU TIP:

In summary, be sure to pull all three copies of your credit reports from each bureau, identify the information you're going to dispute, put a plan in place according to the most important priorities (mentioned in this chapter), and then begin to rebuild your credit with new lines of credit and on-time payments. Keep the credit utilization rate low, and pay off your balances each month.

MALIK DAVIS

CHAPTER 9

Credit Utilization

We've talked about credit utilization a bit in previous chapters, but again, this is your financial manual, so I want you to be able to refer to this information easily.

Here is the gist of this lesson: always stay on top of the of amount of credit you have used compared to how much credit you have been extended by a lender. This is called "credit utilization." This is an important factor in improving and maintaining a good or excellent credit score. Find out how much credit you have available. If your balances are high, start paying down those balances. If you have been making your payments on time every month, the lender may consider you as a good customer and may grant requests to increase your revolving credit lines. As I always tell my clients as an old rule of thumb, keep your credit utilization below thirty percent. I know that I've mentioned this before, but it's worth repeating so that you never forget. Your score won't plummet at thirty-one percent or soar at twenty-nine percent, but basically keep this in mind: the lower the utilization rate, the better the scoring results.

Remaining on point when it comes to credit utilization could be a tough task for some people. Let me put this into perspective for you. Let's say that you only have one credit account and it's a credit card with a limit of $1,000 limit. It's not that hard to hit thirty percent since you'd only need to carry a balance of $300. If you max out that credit card account by charging the entire limit of $1,000, then you should expect your FICO score to drop by ten to forty-five points.

If you have authorized users or joint users on your account, be mindful of the charges they make. If another cardholder maxes out a shared account, both of your FICO scores may fall.

Stay on top of your credit utilization rate by making more than one payment on your debts each month. This will help you if you have to use your credit card on a major expense such as a hefty auto repair bill. Even if you plan to pay off your credit cards relatively quickly, your FICO score may take a hit. It's all about the timing as well. Credit scores are calculated as a snapshot in time, so if you happen to have an engine blow out right after you've charged a new washing machine for $700, your utilization rate will look extremely high.

If you have a high balance, try to pay two-to-three times in a billing cycle, so the billing statement never shows a balance of more than a few hundred dollars. In other words, don't wait for the end of the month to pay down your debt. It's all about timing. Balance this well and your credit score will thank you.

Does this all matter?

Some people may be reading this and thinking, well what does it matter how much I charge as long as I pay my bill on time? If you have too many accounts with balances, it can be a sign that you are a high credit risk. Yet not having any recent credit activity can also be an indicator of increased risk.

In a way, you're damned if you do and damned if you don't. The best tips I can give to achieve a high FICO score by performing well in the credit utilization category are to regularly and responsibly use a few accounts that are different types, pay on time, keep balances low, and only apply for new accounts when you need to mix it up or take advantage of new lines of credit.

CHAPTER 10

Authorized Users

My goal is to give you a variety of options to build and repair your credit, however there are some strategies that I personally stay away from. I've learned NOT to let other people, besides my wife, become authorized users on my accounts. Let's be honest: not everyone is responsible. However, if you have poor credit, and a loving spouse (or someone else) who is willing to allow you to become an authorized user, it can help you out. The term "authorized user" basically means you have someone else's card in your name (or vice versa). You can make purchases with it, but you're not the primary owner of the card. It's an effective way to help establish or reestablish your credit.

While it's certainly not a substitute for building up your own credit history, it is a smart way to give your credit a nice boost as you're getting started. The flip side to being an authorized user on someone's credit card is that your credit can also be hurt if the primary account holder doesn't stay on top of his or her payments. Before deciding if this is right for you, consider the following...

What does it mean to be an authorized user?

Being an authorized user means you can use someone else's credit card in your name. You can make purchases and use the card as if it were your own, but you're not the primary account holder.

To make you an authorized user, the primary account holder simply adds your name to their credit card account, giving you authorization to use it. You'll receive a credit card tied to the account, though you won't have all the privileges of the primary account holder. For example, you probably won't be able to make changes to the account, like requesting a credit line increase or adding more authorized users. As an authorized user, you're not legally responsible to pay the credit card bill or any debts that build up. This is still the primary account holder's responsibility.

How does being an authorized user affect your credit?

Your "authorized user" accounts will likely appear on your credit reports. Most, but not all credit card providers report account activity to an authorized user's credit reports. Before you're added as an authorized user, you may want the primary account holder to ask their credit card provider whether it reports its authorized user accounts to the three major credit bureaus. If the account is reported, the primary account holder's actions could impact your credit for better or for worse. Exactly how much it will affect your credit depends on the scoring model, as different models weigh credit factors differently. For instance

- If the primary account holder has a strong history of on-time payments, this can have a positive impact on your credit.

- Additionally, if the account's credit utilization rate is low, this can also be good for your credit.

- On the other hand, if the primary account holder misses a payment on the card, your credit can plummet— just one late payment can have a severe negative impact. The same goes for high credit utilization on the account.

Who should you ask to add you as an authorized user?

Make sure you select someone you can trust who has healthy credit habits. This includes paying their credit obligations on time and maintaining low credit utilization rates. Think carefully and wisely before you make your decision. Even though there's a potential advantage to being an authorized user, putting yourself on the wrong person's account could have a damaging effect on your scores. A key point to note is that the primary account holder's credit scores will not be affected by adding you as an authorized user, even if your credit history is limited or needs work.

What about becoming a joint account holder?

Some credit card companies may give you the option of opening a joint account. The major difference between being an authorized user and joint account holder is that you have more responsibility as a joint account holder. With a joint account, you are legally responsible to pay off any debts that accumulate.

The process of being added to a joint account is also stricter. Lenders will require joint account holders to meet their conditions as if applying for a single account holder credit card. In most cases, lenders will check the credit for joint account holders. Authorized users usually won't run into this problem, as there's generally no credit check involved.

The authorized user strategy is common for parents who want to help their children build credit. If a parent has established a positive credit history and healthy habits that won't backfire on the child, a parent may want to add a child as an authorized user.

CREDIT GURU TIP:

Think long and hard about becoming or allowing an authorized user!

MALIK DAVIS

CHAPTER 11

All you Need to Know about Credit Profile Numbers

OK so just when you thought you knew it all, let's take this training up a notch. If you want to become your own "Credit Guru" you have to be WELL EDUCATED! There's a popular trend happening now in the credit industry and companies who target vulnerable consumers, the elderly, and even children. Credit Profile Numbers, better known as CPN numbers, credit protection numbers, or secondary credit numbers (SCNs) — are marketed as nine-digit identification numbers that can supposedly be used instead of Social Security Numbers in some instances.

After over twenty years in the credit industry, you'd think I would have seen it all by now, but I still get surprised from time-to-time. Recently, while I was browsing the Internet, I stumbled across this comment that a consumer posted on a popular financial website:

"I have poor credit and I'm not sure what to do. My credit reports have collections, late payments, defaulted accounts and my credit scores are all well below 500. I called a company that I saw online, and they told me about Credit Privacy Numbers and how you can start over by establishing credit using that number instead of your Social Security number. Is that true?"

I've been in the credit industry for over twenty years, and I've seen it all. Unfortunately, in this industry, people tend to think there is a quick fix to bad credit. This leads us to a discussion on "CPN" or credit privacy numbers.

A credit privacy number, also called a credit profile number or CPN, is nine-digit number that can be used to apply for credit. Some credit repair companies will charge a fee to consumers in exchange for a CPN and tell them that this number can be used to secure loans and credit cards. The bait of CPNs (and why many consumers are falling prey to this) is that potential creditors will not have access to a consumer's poor credit upon conducting a credit check. New credit history associated with that number would be reported to the credit bureaus. The consumer gets a clean credit slate with this new number. While it may sound like a sweet deal, there are some serious issues with this.

Consumer Beware

Now, you may be thinking, Malik, why didn't you tell me about this earlier? If it's that easy to bypass my bad credit, sign me up!... PAUSE.

There are several issues, including some that can lead to jail time, associated with CPNs. Major credit bureaus did not just arrive on the scene yesterday, and they will not be fooled by CPNs. Credit Protection Number (CPN) schemes are illegal. There has been a trend happening when a clean credit file is created for a consumer with the intention of fooling the IRS.

Many companies that claim they can clean up credit and/or guarantee a credit score of 700-800 in a short period of time are often involved in CPN schemes. These companies take CPN numbers and run them through public databases such as LexisNexis and SSN Validator to determine their status. If the numbers are clean, meaning they are (validated as an active SSN that is not on file with credit bureaus) they are offered for sale. These are numbers (without credit activity or a positive history) really belong to people in vulnerable situations such as the elderly, children, or those who are incarcerated. Sadly, these people don't have a clue that their numbers are being stolen and sold to consumers. Whether these numbers are called "credit profile number," "credit privacy number" or "credit protection number" (various forms of CPN), don't be fooled; they are really stolen SSNs.

Again, CPN schemes are illegal. Those who purchase a CPN and use it to establish a clean credit file are committing several crimes, including identity theft and making false statements on a loan or credit application. In addition to avoiding CPN numbers, also refrain from using purchased EIN numbers. You cannot replace your EIN number, yet there are various companies who will charge you to do so. Employee Identification Numbers (EIN) are issued by the IRS to identify businesses and people who are self-employed for tax purposes. The only way you can get a new one is to contact the IRS and re-register your company as a new business.

CREDIT GURU TIP:

In general, you will be wise to avoid purchasing CPN, SSN, and EIN numbers. Contact the IRS directly if you want further clarification: 1-800-829-1040.

MALIK DAVIS

CHAPTER 12:

Credit Dispute Letters

Are you ready to take the information that you've used to become your own advocate? All "Credit Gurus" must begin to clean, repair, and build their credit, and now is your time. Remember that accurate information is key when it comes to credit. In addition, if you believe that negative accounts on your credit report cannot be proved to belong to you, you can dispute them. If you don't agree with the information contained on your credit report, send a dispute letter to each of the credit bureaus. You can even dispute any items that you find "questionable."

When you dispute an item, the credit bureaus are obligated by law to investigate your dispute(s). They must either verify, correct, or delete the item from your record within thirty days.

The next section includes sample dispute letters.

CREDIT BUILDING LETTER TEMPLATES

These and additional letters can be found at www.homesteadclt.org

Index of Credit-Rebuilding Letters

Letter #	Letter Should Be Sent to	Reason to Send Letter (Letter Name)
1	Credit Reporting Agency/Bureau	Request for Credit Report
2	Credit Reporting Agency/Bureau	Request for Free Credit Report
3	Credit Reporting Agency/Bureau	Deletions to Credit Report
4	Credit Reporting Agency/Bureau	Corrections to Credit Report
5	Credit Reporting Agency/Bureau	Failure to Respond to Deletion/Correction Letter
6	Credit Reporting Agency/Bureau	Additions to Credit Report
7	Credit Reporting Agency/Bureau	Unauthorized Inquiry
8	Credit Reporting Agency/Bureau	Frivolous-Letter Rejection
9	Credit Reporting Agency/Bureau	Consumer Statement for Disputed Items Following Investigation
10	Credit Reporting Agency/Bureau	Consumer Statement for Disputed Items

11	Credit Reporting Agency/Bureau	Consumer Statement to Make Credit File Complete
12	Credit Reporting Agency/Bureau	Bankruptcy Accounts Not Identified
13	Credit Reporting Agency/Bureau	Request to Update for Completeness of Account History
14	Credit Reporting Agency/Bureau	Mailing-List Restrictions
15	Creditor	Repayment Agreement for Account
16	Creditor	Notice of Overdue Account
17	Creditor	Reduced-Payment Request for Account
18	Creditor	Request for Ceasing Phone Calls
19	Creditor	Proposal to Settle Account
20	Credit Inquirer	Unauthorized Credit Inquiry
21	FTC	Credit Complaint Letter
22	FTC	Predatory Lending Complaint
23	Bureaus	Credit Freeze Letter
24	Debt Collector, CC - Bureaus	Debt Validation Letter
25	Debt Collector	Terms Agreement

[Letter #1]

[Date]

Credit Reporting Agency/Bureau
City, State, Zip
City, State, Zip

RE: REQUEST FOR CREDIT REPORT

To Whom It May Concern:

Please send me a copy of my credit report. My identifying information is as follows:

Name:
SS#:
Address:
City, State, Zip:
Birthdates:

Past residences (last five years):

Former Name(s)

Enclosed is $_____ as payment for the credit report.

If you have any questions, please contact me at (XXX) XXX-XXXX.

Thank you.

Sincerely,

Bruce Smith

CREDIT DISPUTE LETTERS

[Letter #2]

[Date]

Credit Reporting Agency/Bureau
City, State, Zip

RE: REQUEST FOR FREE CREDIT REPORT

To Whom It May Concern:

My credit application was recently denied, and according to the attached letter that I received less than sixty days ago from the company that denied credit to me, your credit bureau issued the report that was used to determine my credit evaluation.

Section 609 [15 USC 1681g] of the Fair Credit Reporting Act of 1970 provides that your credit bureau should send me all information on file that led to my credit application being denied. According to the provisions of Section 612 (b) [15 USC 1681j (b)], there should be no charge for this information.

Please send my credit report to the address below. The attached letter details additional information identifying my account.

If you have any questions or need additional information, please contact me at address noted below.

Thank you.

Sincerely,

John Doe

Address
City, State, Zip
Social Security #

MALIK DAVIS

[Letter #3]

[Date]

Credit Reporting Agency/Bureau
City, State, Zip

RE: DELETIONS TO CREDIT REPORT

To Whom It May Concern:

I received a copy of my credit report and am disputing some items that need to be deleted. I have highlighted and numbered these disputed items on the attached copy. The reasons why these items should be deleted are indicated below:

Item #   Reason for Deletion

According to the provisions of the Fair Credit Reporting Act 611(a) [15 USC 1681i(a)], these disputed items must be reinvestigated or deleted from my credit record within 30 days. During the investigation period, these items must be removed from my credit report as the mere reporting of items prior to debt validation constitutes collection activity. I am also requesting the names, addresses and telephone numbers of individuals you contacted during your investigation.

Please notify me that the above items have been deleted pursuant to 611 (a)(6) [15 USC 1681j (a) (6)]. I am also requesting an updated copy of my credit report, which should be sent to the address listed below. According to the provisions of 612 [15 USC 1681j], there should be no charge for this report.

If you have any questions or need additional information, please contact me at address noted below.

Thank you.

Sincerely,

John Doe
Address
City, State, Zip
Social Security #

MALIK DAVIS

[Letter #4]

[Date]

Credit Reporting Agency/Bureau
City, State, Zip

RE: CORRECTIONS TO CREDIT REPORT

To Whom It May Concern:

I received a copy of my credit report and am disputing some items that need to be corrected. I have highlighted and numbered these disputed items on the attached copy. The reasons why these items should be corrected are indicated below:

Item # Reason for Correction

According to the provisions of the Fair Credit Reporting Act 611(a) [15 USC 1681i(a)], these disputed items must be reinvestigated or deleted from my credit record within 30 days. In the interim, these items should be noted on my credit record as "in dispute." I am also requesting the names, addresses and telephone numbers of individuals you contacted so that I may follow up.

If it is determined through your investigation that the disputed items are inaccurate, please correct my file and send me notification that the information has been updated or deleted. I am requesting an updated copy of my credit report, which should be sent to the address listed below. According to the provisions of 612 [15 USC 1681j], there should be no charge for this report.

If you have any questions or need additional information, please contact me at address noted below.

Thank you.

Sincerely,

John Doe
Address
City, State, Zip
Social Security #

[Letter #5]

[Date]

Credit Reporting Agency/Bureau
City, State, Zip

RE: FAILURE TO RESPOND TO DELETION/CORRECTION LETTER

To Whom It May Concern:

On [insert date of first letter], I sent a letter requesting that you reinvestigate or delete disputed items from my credit report as well as place temporarily remove these items from my report during the investigation period. As of this date, you have failed to respond to my request. A copy of my original letter is attached for your review.

The law stipulates that you must investigate within 30 days of receiving my letter and respond within 5 days of completing your investigation. You have not followed the stipulations of the law.

I may suffer damages because I need to rely on an accurate and complete statement of my credit record and demand that you remove the disputed items from my report immediately as you failed to comply with the law. Otherwise, I will contact the Federal Trade Commission and advise them of your apparent disregard for consumer protection laws.

If you have any questions or need additional information, please contact me at address noted below.

Thank you.

Sincerely,

John Doe
Address
City, State, Zip
Social Security #

_____

[Letter #6]

[Date]

Credit Reporting Agency/Bureau
City, State, Zip

RE: ADDITIONS TO CREDIT REPORT

To Whom It May Concern:

While reviewing a copy my credit report, I discovered that some of my credit references are not included but have been reported. Please add the following accounts along with my credit history as evidenced by the attached letter from the merchant to my credit report.

Merchant Name	Merchant #	Account #

I am requesting an updated copy of my credit report, which should be sent to the address listed below. According to the provisions of 612 [15 USC 1681j] of the Fair Credit Reporting Act, there should be no charge for this report because it currently is incomplete.

If you have any questions or need additional information, please contact me at address noted below.

Thank you.

Sincerely,

John Doe
Address
City, State, Zip
Social Security

MALIK DAVIS

[Letter #7]

[Date]

Credit Reporting Agency/Bureau
City, State, Zip

RE: UNAUTHORIZED INQUIRY

To Whom It May Concern:

I reviewed a copy of my credit report and [company name] ran an unauthorized credit inquiry on me on [date].

I never authorized such action and this constitutes a violation of my rights under the Fair Credit Reporting Act §604 as well as a violation of my rights to privacy. Please contact [company name] and investigate such occurrence.

I am requesting an updated copy of my credit report, which should be sent to the address listed below. According to the provisions of § 612 [15 USC § 1681j], there should be no charge for this report. In addition, as part of your investigation, please send the names, business address and phone numbers of those who made unauthorized credit inquiries so I may contact them directly.

If you have any questions or need additional information, please contact me at address noted below.

Thank you.

Sincerely,

John Doe
Address
City, State, Zip
Social Security

[Letter #8]

[Date]

Credit Reporting Agency/Bureau
City, State, Zip

RE: FRIVOLOUS LETTER REJECTION

To Whom It May Concern:

I am in receipt of your letter stating that my dispute of items in my credit report was "irrelevant and frivolous." I am upset that your credit reporting agency would try such a blatant stall tactic. I am demanding that you reinvestigate my credit file under the Fair Credit Reporting Act Section 611 [15 USC 1681I]. You have no way to ascertain the legitimacy of my action without investigating the items in question.

Enclosed is a copy of my original letter and credit report with the disputed items highlighted. Additional stall tactics on the part of your organization will be reported to the Federal Trade Commission.

If you have any questions, please contact me at the address listed below.

Thank you.

Sincerely,

John Doe
Address
City, State, Zip
Social Security

[Letter #9]

[Date]

Credit Reporting Agency/Bureau
City, State, Zip

RE: CONSUMER STATEMENT FOR DISPUTED ITEMS FOLLOWING INVESTIGATION

To Whom It May Concern:

Your reinvestigation has not resolved my dispute regarding the accuracy and completeness of the highlighted items on my attached credit report. According to the Fair Credit Reporting Act, § 611(b) [USC 15 1681i(b)], I am entitled to "file a statement setting forth the nature of the dispute." I would like potential future creditors to be aware of the dispute, and want the following statement included in my credit report.

[Consumer statement---100 words or less]

I am requesting an updated copy of my credit report which should be sent to the address listed below. According to the provisions of § 612 [15 USC§ 1681j], there should be no charge for this report.

If you have any questions, please contact me at the address listed below.

Thank you.

Sincerely,

John Doe
Address
City, State, Zip
Social Security

MALIK DAVIS

[Letter #10]

[Date]

Credit Reporting Agency/Bureau
City, State, Zip

RE: CONSUMER STATEMENT FOR DISPUTED ITEMS

To Whom It May Concern:

According to the Fair Credit Reporting Act, § 611(b) [USC 15 1681i(b)], I am entitled to "file a statement setting forth the nature of the dispute." I would like potential future creditors to be aware of the dispute, and want the following statement included in my credit report.

[Consumer statement---100 words or less]

I am requesting an updated copy of my credit report, which should be sent to the address listed below. According to the provisions of § 612 [15 USC § 1681j], there should be no charge for this report.

If you have any questions or need additional information, please contact me at (XXX) XXX-XXXX.

Thank you.

Sincerely,

John Doe
Address
City, State, Zip
Social Security

[Letter #11]

[Date]

Credit Reporting Agency/Bureau
City, State, Zip

RE: CONSUMER STATEMENT TO MAKE CREDIT FILE COM-PLETE

To Whom It May Concern:

According to the Fair Credit Reporting Act, § 611(b) [USC 15 1681i(b)], I am entitled to enter a consumer statement in my credit report so that the information is complete and the credit reporting process is fair and equitable to me. I would like the following statement to be made a part of my permanent record so that potential future creditors will be aware of certain circumstances that caused negative credit information.

[Consumer statement-100 words or less]

If you have any questions or need additional information, please contact me at the address listed below.

Thank you.

Sincerely,

John Doe
Address
City, State, Zip
Social Security

MALIK DAVIS

[Letter #12]

[Date]

Credit Reporting Agency/Bureau
City, State, Zip

RE: BANKRUPTCY ACCOUNTS NOT IDENTIFIED

To Whom It May Concern:

I received a copy of my credit report and the items listed below were included in my bankruptcy but are not identified as such on my credit report. Please see the attached copy of the credit report with these item numbers written next to the problem entries as well as a copy of my court documents which lists the creditors included in my bankruptcy.

According to the provisions of the Fair Credit Reporting Act § 611(a) [15 USC 1681i(a)], these disputed items must be updated to reflect discharge in bankruptcy.

I am requesting an updated copy of my credit report, which should be sent to the address listed below. According to the provisions of § 612 [15 USC § 1681j], there should be no charge for this report.

If you have any questions or need additional information, please contact me at the address listed below.

Thank you.

Sincerely,

John Doe
Address
City, State, Zip
Social Security

[Letter #13]

[Date]

Credit Reporting Agency/Bureau
City, State, Zip

RE: REQUEST TO UPDATE FOR COMPLETENESS OF ACCOUNT HISTORY

To Whom It May Concern:

I received a copy of my credit report and am disputing information concerning my payment history. Accordingly, I am requesting that you investigate my dispute and add the attached history of payments to my credit file under the Fair Credit Reporting Act, § 611(a) [15 USC 1681i (a)].

I am requesting an updated copy of my credit report, which should be sent to the address listed below. According to the provisions of § 612 [15 USC § 1681j], there should be no charge for this report. Additionally, if you contact any entity (person or company) in order to make the necessary updates, please provide the names, business address and telephone numbers so that I may follow up directly if needed.

If you have any questions or need additional information, please contact me at the address listed below.

Thank you.

Sincerely,

John Doe
Address
City, State, Zip
Social Security #

[Letter #14]

[Date]

Credit Reporting Agency/Bureau
City, State, Zip

RE: MAILING-LIST RESTRICTIONS

To Whom It May Concern:

I do not wish to have my name, address, telephone number, credit file or other information sold or traded with any marketers. In addition, please do not allow credit issuers to prescreen my credit file for credit offers.

I am requesting that all information about me and my accounts remain private. I want my name, address and credit data excluded from your marketing lists.

Thank you for your assistance with this matter.

Sincerely,

John Doe
Address
City, State, Zip
Social Security

[Letter #15]

[Date]

Creditor   *****SENT VIA CERTIFIED MAIL*****
City, State, Zip

RE: REPAYMENT AGREEMENT FOR ACCOUNT

Dear [name]:

Thank you for speaking with me on [date] regarding my account. As discussed, I have been prompt in paying in the past, but have recently been late due to the following circumstance(s):

I am requesting an amended repayment agreement until my financial situation improves. I would like to pay $[amount] for the next [number] payment periods. After that time, I agree to resume making my full monthly payments.

I understand that during this time I will not be using any credit with [company name].

If my situation changes, I will contact you immediately.

Thank you for your understanding and assistance with this matter. If you have any questions or need additional information, please contact me at the address listed below.

Thank you for your understanding and assistance with this matter. If you have any questions or need additional information, please contact me at the address listed below.

Sincerely,

John Doe
Address
City, State, Zip
Social Security

[Letter #16]

[Date]

Creditor   *****SENT VIA CERTIFIED MAIL*****
City, State, Zip

RE: NOTICE OF OVERDUE ACCOUNT

Dear [name]:

I am aware that my account (#) is overdue, but I have been unable to make payments in a timely manner due to the following circumstances:

My financial difficulties are temporary. I can make a payment by [date]. I will be able to resume my regular payments as of [date]. During this modification period, I respectfully ask that you do not report my payments as late to the credit reporting repositories.

I appreciate you working with me during this difficult time. Your cooperation and understanding is greatly appreciated.

If you have any questions or need additional information, please contact me at the address listed below.

Sincerely,

John Doe
Address
City, State, Zip
Social Security #

[Letter #17]

[Date]

Creditor   *****SENT VIA CERTIFIED MAIL*****
City, State, Zip

RE: REDUCED-PAYMENT REQUEST FOR ACCOUNT

Dear [name]:

I am currently experiencing financial difficulties because [reason].

I have examined my finances and developed a careful budget that includes payment to each creditor. In order to provide for my necessary expenses, I am requesting that each creditor accept a reduced payment until my situation improves with the full understanding that the reduced payment is temporary. In place of my regular payment of [amount], I am requesting that you accept payment of [amount] each month.

I am making every effort to correct my financial situation and expect things to be resolved as of [date]. Until I resume my regular repayments, I will not incur any new debt obligation. Upon your approval, I will immediately remit my first reduced payment.

Thank you for your understanding and cooperation during this difficult time.

If you have any questions or need additional information, please contact me at the address listed below.

Sincerely,

John Doe
Address
City, State, Zip
Social Security #

MALIK DAVIS

[Letter #18]

[Date]

Creditor   *****SENT VIA CERTIFIED MAIL*****
City, State, Zip

RE: REQUEST FOR CEASING PHONE CALLS

Dear [name]:

I have been receiving telephone calls from you concerning my account #. As you have been informed repeatedly, I cannot pay the bill at this time.

Under 15 USCA 1692 c of the Fair Debt Collection Practices Act, this is my formal notice for you to cease all telephone calls except for those permitted by federal law. I am not cutting off communication with your company but rather reduce all communication to writing.

Sincerely,

John Doe
Address
City, State, Zip
Social Security #

[Letter #19]

[Date]

Creditor   *****SENT VIA CERTIFIED MAIL*****
City, State, Zip

RE: PROPOSAL TO SETTLE ACCOUNT

Dear [name]:

Based on our recent discussions, you are aware that I am in financial difficulties because of [reason] and am not currently able to make payments on
my account. My income barely covers my living expenses, and I have no
assets to sell in order to pay you or my other creditors.

I am committed to paying this debt and am willing to offer a settlement of
$_____ as payment in full.

Additionally, I ask that you report this account as "paid in full" and "paid
as agreed" all major credit reporting agencies. I know you have discretion
to report as you deem appropriate so long as consistent with federal law. If
you agree to these conditions, please notify me in writing and I will immediately facilitate payment.

If you have any questions, please contact me at the address listed below.

Sincerely,

John Doe
Address
City, State, Zip

[Letter #20]

[Date]

President *****SENT VIA CERTIFIED MAIL*****
Company
City, State, Zip

RE: UNAUTHORIZED CREDIT INQUIRY

Dear [President's name]

I recently discovered that your company ran an unauthorized report on me on [date]. I did not authorize such an inquiry and demand that you contact [name of credit reporting agency] immediately and have your inquiry deleted from my credit file. You do not have a permissible purpose to pull my credit report hence invaded my right to privacy and may subject to a fine.

If you have any questions, please contact me at the address listed below.

Thank you for your prompt attention to this matter.

Sincerely,

John Doe
Address
City, State, Zip

[Letter #21]

[Date]

Federal Trade Commission
Consumer Response Center
600 Pennsylvania Ave., NW
Washington, DC 20580

RE: CREDIT COMPLAINT LETTER

To Whom It May Concern:

I am writing to file a complaint against [creditor or credit reporting agency].

[Explain situation including name and telephone numbers of people you have spoken to]

Over the past several months, I have tried to resolve this issue, but to no avail. Enclosed is documentation regarding my dealings with [company] to date.

I am requesting your assistance in putting an end to this matter. If you have any questions or need additional information, please contact me at the address listed below.

Thank you for your assistance.

John Doe
Address
City, State, Zip

[Letter #22]

[Date]

Federal Trade Commission
Consumer Response Center
600 Pennsylvania Ave., NW
Washington, DC 20580

RE: PREDATORY LENDING COMPLAINT

To Whom It May Concern:

I am writing to file a complaint against [Loan Company] because of their predatory lending practices.

[Explain situation including name and telephone numbers of people you have spoken to]

I am requesting that you investigate this company and take any appropriate regulatory action, including any necessary referrals to state agencies. It is important that we put an end to these types of deceptive and unethical business practices.

If you have any questions, please contact me at the address listed below.

Thank you for your assistance.

John Doe
Address
City, State, Zip

[Letter 23]

[Date]

[Credit Repository Agency]
Security Freeze
[Address]

RE: CREDIT FREEZE

Dear [Repository]:

I respectfully request a credit freeze on my credit file. My name is [your name].

My former name was (if applicable).

My current address is listed below. My former address was [former address].

My social security number is [social security number].

My date of birth is [date of birth].

I have enclosed photocopies of my state issued identification along with proof of current residence. (Utility bill will suffice).

I have enclosed a fee of $_____ for this service (Please check your state credit freeze laws to determine fee).

Or

I am victim of identity theft and have attached a copy of the investigative report from my local law enforcement agency. Per the laws of the state of [state], I do not have to render a fee for the aforementioned freeze request.

If you have any questions, please contact me at the address listed below.

Thank you for your assistance.

John Doe
Address
City, State, Zip

[Letter 24]

[Date]

[Debt Collector Name] *****SENT VIA CERTIFIED MAIL*****

[Address]

RE: VALIDATION OF ACCOUNT

Account #: [Acct #]

To Whom It May Concern,

I neither affirm, nor deny this purported debt. You claim I owe your company [$].

This letter is being sent to you in response to an entry made on my Credit Report dated [date]. Please be advised that this is not a refusal to pay the debt, but a notice sent pursuant to the Fair Debt Collection Practices Act, 1: USC 1692g Sec 809 (b) that your claim that I owe you money is disputed, and validation is requested.

Under the Fair Debt Collections Practices Act, I have the right to request validation of the debt you say I owe you. I am requesting proof that I am the correct party, and there is some contractual obligation which is binding on me to pay this debt. This is NOT a request for "verification" via E-Oscar or proof of my mailing address, but a request for VALIDATION made pursuant to the above named Title and Section of the Fair Debt Collection Practices Act.

Reporting inaccurate and unsubstantiated information to a credit reporting agency may constitute fraud under federal law. Compliance with this request is required under the laws of state and federal statutes.

Debt validation includes the following:

1. Who was the original creditor on this account, and what was the account number?
2. What was the original amount owed? Please provide a complete payment history, starting with the original creditor.
3. Please provide me documentation that indicates that I agreed to pay someone this sum of money.
4. What was the original date of delinquency for this account?
5. Agreement that grants you the authority to collect on this alleged debt, or proof of acquisition by assignment.
6. What did you pay for this account, and how did you calculate the current amount owed?

I require compliance with the terms and conditions of this letter within 30 days of your certified receipt, or a complete removal from my credit profile, in writing, of your claim. In the event of noncompliance, I reserve the right to file charges and/or complaints with the FTC, and appropriate county, state, and federal authorities. I also hereby reserve my right to take private civil action against your company to recover damages.

In addition, the Fair Credit Reporting Act states that while this item is being investigated you must indicate to the bureau that the account is under dispute and will remove/cease from reporting this information to the Credit Reporting Agency until full validation has been completed.

I have sent a copy of this request for validation to the three national Credit Reporting Agencies to begin their 30-day investigational process concurrent with your investigation.

Sincerely,
John Doe
Address
City, State, Zip
CC: TransUnion, Equifax, Experian

[Letter 25]

[Date]

John Doe

Address

City, State, Zip

RE: TERMS AGREEMENT
(Debt collector acct #/ reference original acct #)

Dear Mr. Smith:

In regards to our verbal agreement to accept settlement of the amount owing on the above described account, please accept this letter as our acceptance of the terms listed below once we have received your payment.

TERMS:

1. [Debt collector name] agrees to accept [$xxx.xx] as payment in full for debt originally owned by [original collector] [original account #] listed under [debt collector name/account number].

2. [Debt collector name] agrees to report this trade line to the three main Credit Repositories/Bureaus as a "Zero Balance" and "Paid as Agreed" account.

3. [Debt collector name] will not give this trade line any new account number, resell this debt or any remaining balance to any other party, re-age the or change the original date of delinquency for this account, or change the reporting status after the terms of the agreement have been met other than the agreement listed in #2 above.

4. (Note to consumer, negotiate for this #4 if possible, however if successful, you will not need terms #2 and #3. Make sure you leave enough time for your delivery method)

[Debt collector name] will remove the account in its entirety as it was reported in error.

This payment must be received by [debt collector] within __ business days of this letter at the address listed below.

Sincerely,

Debt Collector
(Name/title of individual making decision)
Address
City, State

CREDIT GURU TIP:

As you review your credit reports from each bureau, highlight which information you will dispute. Block out a weekend to do nothing but credit repair, including preparing and mailing dispute letters to each bureau. Schedule time each month for the next three to six months to review the status of your disputes and reevaluate your plan and progress to repair your credit.

BONUS CREDIT LETTER TEMPLATES

The letter templates that follow can be found here:

http://www.creditservicer.com/pages/credit-repair/free-sample-letters.php

CREDIT LETTER TEMPLATE

Sample Letter - Request to Cease and Desist

Date:

Name and Address of
Collection Agency:

Re: Account name and number:

You are hereby notified under provisions of Public Law 95-109, Section 805-C, The Fair Debt Collection Practices Act, to hereby CEASE and DESIST in all attempts to collect the above debt.

This letter is your legal notice under the above mentioned federal law that regulates the activities of collection agencies and their legal representatives.

Your failure to Cease and Desist, as directed in this letter, will result in charges being filed against you with the state and federal regulatory agencies empowered with the enforcement of this law.

You are further warned that NO derogatory information is to be placed on any credit reports after receipt of this notice, or that action will result in further charges being filed against you.

It is my firm decision not to recognize or work with any collection agency. I will settle this affair directly with the original creditor.

Please give this legal notice your full attention.

Sincerely,

(Your Name)
(Address)
(Date of Birth)
(Social Security Number)

Sample Letter - Request to Add a Consumer Statement

Date:

Name and Address of
Credit Bureau

Re: Adding a Consumer Statement

Dear Sir / Madam:

According to the Fair Credit Reporting Act (FCRA), I have the right to enter a "Consumer Statement" in my credit report. I have disputed the accuracy and completeness of certain items on my credit report, and since reinvestigation has not resolved my dispute, I want the following statement, without alteration, placed in the file.

"Your message here"

I assume that 30 days constitutes reasonable time for completing this update, unless you notify me otherwise. Please send an updated copy of my credit report containing this statement to the address shown below.

Sincerely,

(Your Name)
(Address)
(Date of Birth)
(Social Security Number)

Sample Letter - Request Removal of Inquiries

(Name and Address of Creditor or Lender)

Re: Unauthorized Credit Inquiry

Dear (Name of Creditor or Lender),

I recently received a copy of my Experian credit report. The credit report showed a credit inquiry by your company that I do not recall authorizing. I understand that you shouldn't be allowed to put an inquiry on my file unless I have authorized it. Please have this inquiry removed from my credit file because it is making it very difficult for me to acquire credit.

I have sent this letter certified mail because I need your prompt response to this issue. Please be so kind as to forward me documentation that you have had the unauthorized inquiry removed.

If you find that I am remiss, and you did have my authorization to inquire into my credit report, then please send me proof of this.

Thanking you in advance,

(Your Name)
(Address)
(Date of Birth)
(Social Security Number)

Sample Letter - Explanation of Delinquent Account

Date:

Name and Address of
Credit Agency

Re: Explanation of Delinquent Account Number _____

Dear Creditor:

It has recently come to my attention that several of my payments to the above referenced account have been labeled "late" on my credit report.

I have been prompt in paying in the past, and missed the payments due to: "Explain here"

Since these late payments occurred for an excusable reason, please correct the payment history for my account at the following credit bureaus:
____Experian
____TransUnion
____Equifax

It is important that my credit report reflect the good relations I have had with your company in the past. In addition, the requested corrections will make the report more representative of my financial habits.

Sincerely,

(Your Name)
(Address)
(Date of Birth)
(Social Security Number)

Sample Letter - Request a Free Credit Report (1)

Date:

(Name of credit bureau)
(Address of credit bureau)

Please send me a copy of my credit report.

> My full name is:
> My social security number is:
> My birthdate is:
> My current address is:
> My previous address is:

I may have received credit in the last five years under the following names:

Enclosed is a copy of my driver's license as proof of my name and address.

I am making this request for a free credit report since I have been denied credit in the last 60 days based on one of your reports. A copy of the denial letter is attached for your information.

Sincerely,

(Your Name)

Sample Letter - Request a Free Credit Report

Date:

(Name of credit bureau)
(Address of credit bureau)

Re: Request for a Free Credit Report

To whom it may concern:

According to the attached letter, which states that my credit application was denied, your credit bureau was reported to have been used in the evaluation of my credit.

The Fair Credit Reporting Act, amended July 1999, provides that you send me a copy of the information used, which led to the denial of my application. According to this provision there should be no charges for this information.

Please send me a copy of the requested credit report to the address shown below. I have enclosed a copy of my driver's license to show proof of my identity and place of residence.

Sincerely,

(Your Name)
(Address)
(Date of Birth)
(Social Security Number)

CREDIT LETTER TEMPLATES

Sample Letter - Request for an Investigation (1)

Date:

(Name of credit bureau)
(Address of credit bureau)

Attn: Consumer Relations
Re:
(Your Name)
(Your credit report ID #)
(Your address)
(Your telephone #)
(Your social security #)
(Your date of birth)

Please begin an investigation of the following items listed on my credit report that are reported inaccurately.

Creditor: _____

Account #: _____

Reason for dispute: _____

Please update my credit report and send me a copy at the conclusion of your investigation. In addition, send the results to the three major credit bureaus: Experian, Equifax, and Trans Union.

Thank you for your help and prompt attention to this matter.

Respectfully,

(Your Name)

Sample Letter - Request an Investigation (2)

Date:

(Name of credit bureau)
(Address of credit bureau)

Re: Request for an Investigation

To Whom It May Concern:

Recently, I received a copy of my credit profile and found the following accounts are being reported incorrectly.

ABC Credit Union - Account # 123-456-789 This is not my account. Please investigate, verify and delete.

ABC Department Store - Account # 123-456-789 This is not my account. Please investigate, verify and delete.

Please send the updated credit report to the following address:

(Your Name)
(Address)
(Date of Birth)
(Social Security Number)

Sample Letter - Dispute Letter to a Creditor

Date:

(Name of creditor or lender)
(Address of creditor or lender)
Re:
(Your Name)
(Your address)
(Your account number)

To whom it may concern:

I have recently obtained a credit report from (credit bureau). It shows the above account with your company was (days late, charged-off, other problems, etc.) To the best of my knowledge, I have always paid this account promptly and satisfactorily. This incorrect information is seriously hurting my credit rating, and I would appreciate it if you would verify this information and correct it with all three credit bureaus. If the information cannot be verified, please delete the account from my credit report.

Please inform me with the results of your verification as soon as possible. Your immediate attention to this matter is greatly appreciated.

Sincerely,

(Your Name)

Sample Letter - Request a Merge Inquiry

Date:

Name and Address of Credit Bureau

Re: Request to Merge Inquiry with Account

Dear Sir / Madam:

I recently received my credit report and found problems of inaccurate reporting. A copy of the credit report is attached, with the items marked.

The presence of the inquiries as entries separate from the resulting account inaccurately duplicates information. The inquiries also reflect an incomplete and inaccurate processing of information in my file. The inquiry entries should be removed, or at least merged into the accounts to which they belong.

Under the provisions of the Fair Credit Reporting Act (FCRA), amended July 1999, please investigate and delete these disputed items. I will assume that 30 days constitutes reasonable time to complete this request, unless you notify me otherwise. It should be understood that failure to verify within this time constitutes non-verification, and the items must be promptly deleted according to the provisions of the FCRA.

Please send me a copy of the requested credit report to the address shown below.

Sincerely,

(Your Name)
(Address)
(Date of Birth)
(Social Security Number)

Sample Letter - Reminder to Respond (1)

Date:

Name and Address of Credit Bureau

Re: Reminder to Respond

Dear Sir / Madam:

Thirty days ago I sent you a letter disputing certain items on my credit report which were inaccurate or incomplete. Attached is the original letter.

Please note that under the provisions of the Fair Credit Reporting Act (FCRA), 30 days is considered as reasonable time for responding to my request for verification of the disputed items, unless additional time is requested by your firm in writing. In addition, failure to verify these items within the 30-day period, constitutes reason to drop them from my file, pursuant to sections 623(a)(1)(b) and 623(a)(3) of the FCRA.

Please respond immediately so that I do not need to pursue my legal rights under the FCRA, which requires your compliance with the law.

Also, please send me a copy of the requested credit report to the address shown below.

Sincerely,

Your Name
Address
Date of Birth
Social Security Number

Sample Letter - Reminder to Respond (2)

Date:

(Name of credit bureau)
(Address of credit bureau)

Attn: Consumer Relations

To whom it may concern:

On (date of investigation request), I sent you a request to investigate certain items on my credit report that I believe to be incorrect or inaccurate. As of today, (# of weeks you waited) have passed, and I have not yet received a response from you. Under the Fair Credit Reporting Act, you are required to respond, "within a reasonable time." If the information cannot be verified, please delete it from my credit report. I would appreciate your immediate attention in this matter. Please inform me of the results.

Sincerely,

(Your Name)
(Address)
(Date of Birth)
(Social Security Number)

Sample Letter - Settlement of Account

Date:

Name and Address of
Credit Bureau

Re: Settlement of Account Number _____

Dear Creditor:

This letter is to confirm our telephone conversation on _____ regarding the settlement of the above account.

As discussed, I will pay your company the amount of $_____ as full settlement of this account.

Please respond immediately so that I do not need to pursue my legal rights under the FCRA, which requires your compliance with the law.

Also, please send me a copy of the requested credit report to the address shown below.

Sincerely,

(Your Name)
(Address)
(Date of Birth)
(Social Security Number)

Sample Letter - Request to Update Your Credit Report

Date:

Name and Address of
Credit Bureau

Re: Request to Update Credit Report

Please note that under the provisions of the Fair Credit Reporting Act (FCRA), you are obligated to delete obsolete information from my consumer credit report.

Please refer to the information highlighted on the attached copy of my report. It is obsolete and should be deleted immediately from your credit files.

Pursuant to provisions of the FCRA, I am entitled to notification that the items have been deleted. Please send an updated copy of my credit report to the address shown below, as well as to any other party that has inquired about my credit rating in the last six months.

Sincerely,

(Your Name)
(Address)
(Date of Birth)
(Social Security Number)

Sample Letter - Goodwill Letter

Date:

Sears NAAC
ATTN : Credit Bureau Desk
ABC Street
City, State, Zip

Regarding: Account No. XXXXXXX

To Whom It May Concern:

I am writing a letter about my experience with Sears that is a mixture of a grateful "thank-you" and a pressing request concerning a Sears Charge Card trade line in my credit files that I would like to have revised.

I received the Sears card in [YEAR], several years before I [CHAOTIC LIFE EVENT -- A MOVE, A BIRTH, MEDICAL SICKNESS, ETC.]. Later when I experienced the [CHAOTIC LIFE EVENT] and while working on [WORK PROJECT], I became disorganized with respect to, as you saw, making timely payments with Sears. I fully recognize my responsibility with respect to payable accounts and have worked diligently to rehabilitate my relationship with Sears since that time.

To be honest, that year was a "wake-up" call for me regarding fiscal organization. Since then I believe I have learned the essential organizational and financial management principles I desperately needed at that point. Thankfully, responsible credit management is now reflected in my credit records which -- excluding the Sears card late entry -- are excellent. I wish to thank you for renewing your confidence in me and for giving me a second chance at a relationship with you, one that I am determined to keep spotless.

We are about to shop for a mortgage, and it has come to my attention that the late notations from Sears may preclude me from taking full advantage of the very lowest interest rates now available. Since those notations do not reflect my current status with Sears, I am requesting that you give me a second chance at a positive credit rating by revising those trade lines. Your customer service representative suggested that I write you for a "goodwill adjustment." I sincerely hope that there is redemption at Sears, and I beg you for such consideration. Please let me know if any additional documentation would assist in reaching a positive outcome, and I thank you again for the time you have spent reading this letter.

Very hopefully yours,

Name
Address
City, STATE ZIP

CREDIT BUREAU CONTACT INFORMATION

EQUIFAX

Equifax Mailing Address
Equifax Credit Information Services, LLC
P.O. Box 740241, Atlanta, GA 30374

Equifax Phone Numbers:
866-349-5186: Dispute Credit Report Items
800-685-1111: Request Free Credit Report
888-766-0008: Place Fraud Alert on Profile
866-493-9788: Existing Customer Support
888-202-4025: Business Solutions
404-885-8078: Fax Number

EXPERIAN

Experian Mailing Address
Experian National Consumer Assistance Center
P.O. Box 4500, Allen, TX 75013

Experian Phone Numbers:
800-509-8495: Dispute Credit Report Items
888-397-3742: Report Requests & Fraud Help
877-284-7942: Existing Customer Support
888-243-6951: Business Credit Services
972-390-4908: Fax Line

CHAPTER 13:

Final Tips to Break the Chains of Bad Credit

The middle of the tunnel is always the darkest, the loneliest, and the most challenging. It may be tempting to quit as you're on the journey to financial freedom. When those moments arise, reflect on how far you've come. You've invested in yourself by purchasing this book. By now, your mental wheels are spinning and you're already thinking of what needs to be done first. Perhaps you've pulled your credit reports, have begun making notes, sending letters, and disputing errors. That takes work, and to see the results will take time. Continue to move forward and remember that you do have the power to *Break the Chains*. I did. I climbed out of the tunnel where I started, fought my way from a life of poverty to a life of freedom, and you can too. No more bondage. No more limits, and no more chains.

Keep these credit repair tips in mind as you work toward a better credit score and a financial future.

1.   **Salvage.** Make all your payments on time, and prioritize your good-standing accounts over collections and other debts. Don't sacrifice accounts that are in good standing for accounts that are not.

2.   **Spread**. You may have several items to dispute and that's fine. My recommendation is to put three to five in each letter and space out your disputes. Credit bureaus could become suspicious of too many disputes and consider them frivolous.

3.   **Don't close**. Rarely does closing a credit card help your credit score. Remember what we've covered in this book; closing a credit card is more likely to hurt your credit score especially when the account has a balance.

4.   **No self-inflicted pain**. In this book, we've discussed the behaviors and factors that hurt your credit score. Now there is no excuse. Go back and review the items that have a negative impact on your credit score so you can avoid making more mistakes. There's no need to commit credit suicide, when your credit can help you live an abundant life.

5.   **Don't be discouraged by setbacks**. Credit repair may feel like a roller coaster at first. Your credit score may drop and then increase and drop again as you go through the process. This doesn't necessarily mean you've done something wrong. Continue adding positive information to your credit report and your credit score will improve over time. Patience will be a key virtue.

6.   **Get consumer credit counseling or credit repair services**. If your debts are overwhelming, creditors aren't willing to work with you, and you

can't seem to come up with a payment plan on your own, consumer credit counseling is an option for getting back on track. Remember, I can also help you with credit repair. Visit www.yourcreditguru.net learn about my latest programs.

7.   **If bankruptcy is inevitable, file sooner rather than later.** Again, I'm not a proponent of bankruptcy. I believe you should attempt to negotiate and prioritize, however, if filing bankruptcy is the only way you can get back on track, don't waste time on investing in what will not work. Evaluate whether you should file for bankruptcy early, so you can start the process and begin to rebuild your life.

REFERENCES

Below are the financial resources mentioned and sourced in this book. Educate yourself on all things credit so that you can truly live the life you desire.

- www.Yourcreditguru.net
- AnnualCreditReport.com
- MyFico.com
- VantageScore.com
- TheScore.VantageScore.com
- Debt.org
- CreditKarma.com
- CreditSesame.com
- NavyFederal.org
- Inc.com
- Wallethub.com
- Homesteadclt.org
- Usatoday.com/money
- www.MalikDavis.com

CONGRATULATIONS!

You've reached the end, and I want to thank you for reading this book. Most importantly, I want to congratulate you, as you've just completed a crash course in credit repair. You are now one more step closer to achieving the financial freedom you desire and becoming your own Credit Guru. Treat this book like your financial bible. If after reading and studying the material here, you still require my assistance, contact me any time via email at realtopcreditguru@gmail.com.

ABOUT THE AUTHOR

Malik Davis is a financial credit consultant with over twenty years in the financial services business. He is a mentor to entrepreneurs and credit consultants and the go-to credit guru for today's celebrities. Over the span of his career, he has helped thousands of individuals regain their financial freedom and change their lives. Often, people come to Mr. Davis with credit scores of less than 600 and within a short time frame, their scores increase to over 750. He is an expert at removing blemishes and inaccurate, erroneous information from consumer credit files. By improving consumer credit reports, Malik Davis empowers families, individuals, and communities to Break the Chains of financial despair. Learn more and get started at www.MalikDavis.com and www.YourCreditGuru.net.

Did Break The Chains help you in your financial journey? Don't forget to leave a review on Amazon.com and to share this book title with someone you know.

52109663R00104

Made in the USA
San Bernardino, CA
05 September 2019